MURDER *by* CANDLELIGHT

MURDER *by* CANDLELIGHT

The Gruesome Crimes Behind
Our Romance with the Macabre

MICHAEL KNOX BERAN

PEGASUS CRIME

NEW YORK LONDON

MURDER BY CANDLELIGHT

Pegasus Books LLC
80 Broad Street, 5th Floor
New York, NY 10004

ISBN: 978-1-60598-820-7

10 9 8 7 6 5 4 3 2 1

Printed in the United States of America

Distributed by W. W. Norton & Company, Inc.

Very few can boast of hearts which they dare lay open to themselves, and of which, by whatever accident exposed, they do not shun a distinct and continued view. . . .

—*Dr. Johnson*

Contents

Romantic Murder

> Lately I have found it a nocturnal refuge to read
> books of the early and middle nineteenth century:
> Skeats's edition of Chatterton, Dickens's *Life of
> Grimaldi*, Collins and Cruikshank's *Punch and
> Judy*, Dyce's edition of Beaumont and Fletcher. . . .
> I like the atmosphere of English antiquities, the
> Gothic churches and the slang of old London, the
> clotted and cobwebbed prose . . . the murkiness
> and tangledness of texts that leave so much of the
> past mysterious.
>
> —*Edmund Wilson*

In his essay "The Decline of the English Murder," George Orwell opined that the classic period of English homicide began about 1850 and died away circa 1925. Reading the piece some years ago, I found myself inclined to disagree. Orwell conceived the classic murderer to be, like Dr. Palmer of Rugeley, Major Armstrong of Cusop Dingle, and that curious figure Dr. Crippen, a respectable, middle-class figure, the follower, perhaps, of a learned profession, who brings about the death of an inconvenient person by means of poison. But surely the hygienic, frock-coated neatness of Orwell's classic murders, so far from marking them as masterpieces of the genre, was indicative of a degeneration of the form, the triumph of a bloodless, attenuated species of killing over the wilder and more impassioned varieties, with all their sanguinary élan. Also, the victim of a poisoner is often unaware that he or she is being murdered, a circumstance which deducts materially from the amount of horror such a case can excite.

Like a diamond, a murder shows best by candlelight. It seems to me that the age when murder was most "classical"—that is, when it was most macabre—fell somewhat earlier than Orwell would have us think. The golden age of murder (if it is not unseemly to use such an expression in connection with such a subject) is, I am convinced, to be found in and around the quarter-century that elapsed between 1811 and 1837, an era bounded on the one side by the commencement of the regency of Prince George, afterwards King George IV, and on the other by the accession of his niece, Queen Victoria.

But how to justify this, what is to my thinking the *saeculum aureum* of murder, its Age of Gold? Certainly the atmosphere of the period has something to do with it, the ghastly, Gothic, and peculiarly English quality of an age in which candlelight gave way to gaslight and the mail coach to railways—an age of chop-houses and hackney coaches, when watchmen called "Charlies" cried the hours of the night and young harlots cursed like sailors in streets daubed with the soot of hell. Other ages, however, have scenes as ghastly to show; and if the murders of this period seem to me to have been especially lurid, the reason is perhaps to be found less in the acts themselves than in the impression they made, at the time, on sensitive and imaginative minds. It is less the quality of the crimes than the attitude of the age which determines the gruesomeness of its murders.

The killings described in this book took place in the high noon of Romanticism, when the most vital spirits were in revolt against the eighteenth-century lucidity of their fathers and grandfathers, those powdered, periwigged gentlemen who had been bred up in the sunshine of the Enlightenment, and who were as loath to descend to the Gothic crypt as they were to contemplate the Gothic skull beneath the skin. The Romantic Age, by contrast, was more than a little in love with blood and deviltry. It was an age that delighted in the clotted gore of the seventeenth-century dramatists, the bloody poetry of Webster and Tourneur and Middleton. "To move a horror skillfully," Charles Lamb wrote in his 1808 book *Specimens of English Dramatic Poets Who Lived about the Time of Shakespeare*, "to touch a soul to the quick, to lay upon fear as much as it can bear, to wean and weary a life till it is ready to drop, and then step in with mortal instruments to take its last forfeit: this only a Webster can do." Inferior geniuses, Lamb said, may "terrify babes with painted devils," but they "know not how a soul is to be moved."

The keenest spirits of this epoch in murder history—Sir Walter Scott, Thomas De Quincey, and Thomas Carlyle among them—knew a good deal about the horror that moves the soul. In their contemplations of the most notorious murders of their time, they saw "strange images of death" and discovered dreadfulnesses in the act of homicide that we, in an age in which murder has been antiseptically reduced to a problem of social science on the one hand and skillful detective work on the other, are only too likely to have overlooked.

For the student of history, the murders of a vanished time have this other value. An eminent historian has said that were he limited, in the study of a particular historical period, to one sort of document only, he would choose the records of its murder trials as being the most comprehensively illuminating. A history of the murders of an age will in its own way reveal as much of human nature, caught in the Minotaur-maze of evil circumstance, as your

Horror's Romance: From the Gothic Donjon to the Metropolitan Blood-Sacrifice

A corpse, a bloody piteous corpse,
Pale, pale as ashes, all bedaubed in blood,
All in gore-blood. . . .

         —*Shakespeare*

Al over England, people were looking to be scared out of their wits. The rage for being frightened to death began in the middle of the eighteenth century, when, in the high noon of the Age of Reason, Horace "Horry" Walpole, dilettante son of the Whig Prime Minister Sir Robert, grew bored of neo-classical sweetness and light. He was from an early age drawn to Gothic corpses and cobwebbery, and in 1764 he published, under a pen name, a novel called *The Castle of Otranto*, in which he whimsically evoked the very Gothic ghoulishness the reformers of his time were trying to forget.

The book created a new appetite, and England was soon awash in shudder novels. Tiring of the orderly parterres of Pope and Dr. Johnson, readers were drawn to the wilder literary gardens of such writers as Ann Radcliffe and William Beckford. Books like Mrs. Radcliffe's *The Mysteries of Udolpho*, in which the innocent heroine is cruelly immured in an Italian castle, and Beckford's *Vathek*, the story of the descent of an eastern potentate into a lurid hell, offered the reader glimpses of the exotic and the forbidden, and at the same time satisfied his craving for romances in which the sensuous and voluptuous passions were artfully mingled with the vicious and depraved ones.

Horror, after all, is scarcely horror without a tincture of warped eroticism, and as a rule the Gothic novelists laid their tales in the Gothic castle, and more especially in the Gothic donjon. Their readers ate it up, for they instinctively associated the castle with the more blood-curdling varieties of vice and licentious deviancy. A very pardonable assumption: castle pride has long been closely interwoven with castle perversity. From Caligula to Colonel Charteris, the "Rape-Master General of Britain," the castle has been the locus classicus of erotic horror. The Marquis de Sade himself, blond scion of the Frankish knightage which in the Dark Ages gave aristocracy to Europe, could never have existed but for the rank luxuriance of his château, with its hereditary right of domination; the feudal morbidities of the marquis who made a fetish of his pedigree were the whip and spur of the manias that drove the zealot of sadistic copulation.

In time, however, the Gothic formulas grew stale, and by 1817 the Gothic castle, with its trapdoors and spy-holes cut out of the eyes of ancestral portraits, had become insipid. In that year, Jane Austen published *Northanger Abbey*, a novel in which she mocked the Gothic genre as unreal. "Charming as were all Mrs. Radcliffe's works," she wrote, "and charming even as were the works of all her imitators, it was not in them, perhaps, that human nature, at least in the midland counties of England, was to be looked for."

Another assault, far more comprehensive than that of the eighteenth-century Gothicists, was by this time under way against the complacencies of the Age of Reason. A new generation had arisen to seek what Cardinal Newman called "a deeper philosophy" of the soul. The Romantic rebels sought to penetrate the depths of human nature less by means of analytical intelligence than through feeling and force of soul; and indeed one of their number, the East Prussian sage Johann Georg Hamann, went so far as to say that only "love—for a person or an object—can reveal the true nature of anything."

The Romantics brought this ideal of sympathetic insight to bear on nearly every aspect of human life. In politics and statecraft, the Romantic revolution was inaugurated by Edmund Burke, who taught his disciples to perceive the hidden beauty of ancient customs and institutions, and to dread the "new conquering empire of light and reason" that threatened to destroy them. William Wordsworth ushered in a corresponding revolution in poetry, inculcating through his poems qualities of feeling and sentiment at odds with the artificiality of a society which he believed had grown deaf to the mystic language of nature and truth. Not less valuable was the Romantic effort to understand the nature of evil and to reinstate it in all its dark majesty as a fact of the human soul. To be sure, not a few of the Romantic poets dallied, in the first ebullience of youth, with the belief that man is born good and corrupted by institutions; but the push and thrust of the movement was always toward a recognition that sin is real and ineradicable. The demon-lovers of Samuel Taylor Coleridge's poems, the witches and gremlins and occult *gramayre* (magic) that haunted Sir Walter Scott's imagination, the young Thomas Carlyle's Diogenes Teufelsdröckh ("Devilsdung"), the protagonist of the dark fantasy *Sartor Resartus*, all bear witness to the Romantic conviction that the devil lives in each of us, feeding on the worms that fester in the vitals of our spirit.

"He hath a demon," the essayist William Hazlitt said of George Gordon Byron, sixth Baron Byron. Inferior, as a poet, to Coleridge and Wordsworth, and the author of reams of verse that largely bore the modern reader, Lord Byron was yet more scrupulous than his poetical coevals in his investigations of human nastiness. He resembled nothing so much as one of the holy fanatics of Russia who believed that if they were to know the truth of evil, they must descend in their own persons to the lowest pits of depravity. Byron could scarcely bear to be outstripped in the competition for malignant experience. The French writer Chateaubriand had been beguiled by a dream of incest; Byron must out-scandal him by making love to his half-sister, Augusta Leigh. The eighteenth-century *roué* Sir Francis Dashwood had instituted a mock religious order, the Friars of St. Francis of Wycombe, consecrated to voluptuous debauchery; Byron must surpass him by establishing, at Newstead Abbey, his own Order of the Skull, and by drinking claret from a defunct human cranium. Casanova had, in a long career of incessant ribaldry, shown himself a notable son of Priapus; Byron, at Venice, must try to out-wench him, with what success we cannot be sure.

As the man, so the verse. It is morbid. "The flowers that adorn his poetry," Hazlitt writes, "bloom over charnel-houses and the grave." And yet there was a deeper stratum of horror that Byron could not penetrate, assiduously though he tried. In June 1816, having exiled himself from a too-respectably bourgeois England, he was living in the Villa Diodati at Lake Geneva. His friend, the poet Percy Bysshe Shelley, had taken a house nearby and, during a long spell of rain, Shelley and his traveling companions—Mary Godwin, the young lady who was soon to become his wife, and her stepsister Claire, Byron's girlfriend at the time—spent much time in the Villa Diodati. Byron's physician, John William Polidori (a lugubrious young man whom Stendhal mistook for the poet's pimp) recalled how one evening about midnight the group "really began to talk ghostly." A volume of German horror stories lay to hand, and the wine and laudanum (opium) flowed freely. At one point, Byron recited part of Coleridge's poem *Christabel.* The innocent Christabel, having undressed and gotten into bed, is reclining on her elbow as her new-found friend Lady Geraldine (who is in fact a *lamia,* or anthropophagic demon) begins to disrobe:

> *Then drawing in her breath aloud,*
> *Like one that shuddered, she unbound*
> *The cincture from beneath her breast:*
> *Her silken robe, and inner vest,*
> *Dropt to her feet, and in full view,*
> *Behold! her bosom and half her side—*
> *Hideous, deformed, and pale of hue—*
> *O shield her! shield sweet Christabel!*

The silence that followed was broken when Shelley, "suddenly shrieking and putting his hands to his head, ran out of the room with a candle." He afterwards said that as he listened to Coleridge's lines, he "thought of a woman he had heard of who had eyes instead of nipples."

The participants in the synod in the Villa Diodati agreed that each would write a ghost story. Byron began to compose a vampire tale, but he soon tired of it. Polidori turned the fragment into a novella, *The Vampyre,* in which his cloven-footed patron (Byron had a clubfoot) figures as the bloodsucking villain. Touché! But in other respects *The Vampyre* was a weak book, and Byron himself was soon absorbed in the composition of another work, his dramatic poem *Manfred.* But like the other Byronic heroes—like Count Lara, the Corsair, and the Giaour— Manfred is merely a facsimile of Byron himself: he can disturb no one's sleep. His pose is worse than his bite; he is yet another villain on the model of Mrs. Radcliffe's Montoni, the more tedious, as he mopes about the alpine peaks, on account of his penchant for extended soliloquies in which he ponders his own mysterious agony and laments the untimely death of his sister, Astarte. ("I loved her, and destroy'd her.")

Of all the books produced under the inspiration of the symposium in the Villa Diodati, only Mary Godwin's *Frankenstein** represented a real advance in the quest for a subtler horror, a truer Gothic. This was because she grounded her castle more firmly in reality than the other Gothic writers did theirs. She converted her demonic hero into a modern laboratory scientist, and she portrayed his diabolic progeny—the monster himself—as a rebel against an oppressive social order, ready to stand at the next by-election in the Radical interest. Yet it was not Mary but her seducer, Shelley himself, who in 1816 bid fair to be the new master of the macabre. A butterfly spirit, the poet had abandoned his first wife, Harriet, to run away, in 1814, with Mary, who was then a girl of sixteen. He was from an early age preoccupied with witches, sprites, and demons, and he grew up "a kind of ghastly object, colourless, pallid, without health, or warmth, or vigour; the sound of him shrieky, frosty, as if a ghost were trying to sing. . . ." As he matured, Shelley became conscious of realms of experience that seemed to him to lie beyond the limits of ordinary sense-perception, and he was bedeviled by mental phantoms that haunted him like "vampire bats before the glare of the tropic sun"—nightmarish visions of friends lacerated, a wife strangled, a dead child reanimated.

But Shelley never found a literary form that adequately conveyed the peculiar terror he felt merely in being alive. The "foul fiends," "pale snakes," and "semivital worms" of his poems are growths of the Gothic hothouse; they haunt a world too different from the one we know to make us afraid in the way he was afraid. His horror-poetry is in its own way as unreal as the horror-prose

---

*   By the time the book was completed, Mary had wed Shelley: the volume was published anonymously in London in 1818.

of Mrs. Radcliffe and William Beckford; in it we find the same old Gothic castle, only now perceived hallucinogenically.*

———•———

Shelley drowned in 1822 when his sailboat sank in the Gulf of Spezia; Byron died two years later at Missolonghi, where he had gone to help the Greek patriots in their struggle against the Turks. The breakthrough that eluded the Romantic poets would instead be made by their cousins, the Romantic prose-masters—by writers who, like the two Toms, Thomas De Quincey and Thomas Carlyle, found the essence of horror not in the castle, that fabulous and remote place, but in the real if commonplace streets of the modern city. They saw that the daily life of the metropolis, if studied closely and sympathetically, yielded scenes as strange, as pregnant with mysterious terror, as the myths and romances on which the Romantic poets fed. Nowhere did the prose-masters come closer to distilling the essence of this living Gothicism than in their studies of the modern blood-sacrifice, that crime with the "primal eldest curse" upon it, the living hell of the modern metropolitan murder.

---

* Shelley's hallucinogenic vision may have been heightened by an encounter with the tenth muse, Syphilis. Shelley was convinced that he had contracted the disease when he was a student at Oxford, and he told Leigh Hunt that the memory of this tainted lust inspired the lines in *Epipsychidion* in which he describes an enchantress "whose voice was venomed melody," whose touch was "electric poison."

PART ONE

The Murder in the Dark Lane

This lane is a d—d nasty dark place; as dark
as the grave.

—*Jack Thurtell*

CHAPTER ONE

The Body in the Brook

Horrible thoughts of death, and shrouds with blood
upon them, and a fear that has made me burn as if
I was on fire, have been upon me all day.

—*Dickens*

On an autumn day in 1823, a coach set out from the town of Watford, in Hertfordshire, and drove toward the nearby village of Elstree, some ten miles north of London. "That is the place," a voice said. The coach came to a halt near a brook called Hill Slough; as the occupants alighted, it was evident from the expression on their faces that they were looking for something. With rake, fish-fork, drag, and Indian ladder, they searched the waters of Hill Slough. At last, in the deepest part of it, they found something and drew it up with a grapple. It was a large sack—just under six bushels. The lower extremities of a human corpse protruded from it: its feet were crossed at the ankles and tied with a cord.

The sack was brought ashore; the body, when taken out, looked as though it had lain in the water for some time. With the exception of a red shawl, which had been tied around the neck and filled with stones, the body was naked; and there were marks of violence about the head and face. The right cheek had been pierced clean through; the throat had been cut; and the skull had been broken open to reveal the brains, in which fragments of skull-bone had become stuck.

———·———

The story behind the corpse in the brook at Hill Slough is a story of murder. For "cold-blooded villainy," *The Times* opined shortly after the body was found, the crime was one that had "seldom been equalled." There was a "ferocity" in it that had "awakened the drowsy sensations of the world into feelings of horror." As usual in such cases, the public was at once appalled and secretly delighted by an episode that promised to interrupt what *The Times* called "the dull uniformity of civil life." A hundred newspapers followed the story closely; innumerable books, chapbooks, pamphlets, and broadsides were printed and sold; plays dramatizing the crime were put on in London theaters; and penny peep shows re-enacting it were performed at market fairs. *The Times* itself, a little defensive, perhaps, on account of its own extensive coverage of the case, said that it would "offer no apology for presenting" its readers with the most minute particulars connected with the "dreadful event."

For much of the nineteenth century, the murder of the man fished out of Hill Slough was a byword for depravity, its status as a *cause célèbre* secured by the lurid impressions it left upon the English mind. The naked body, stuffed into its coarse shroud and thrown into the water; the groans and strange cries that were heard in the nearby village of Radlett after sunset on the Friday before the body was recovered; the revelation that the killing was connected with secretive figures in the London underworld—such were the circumstances of the crime that its horror could not easily be overlooked. Indeed, it was the fascination the case exercised over such figures as Lord Macaulay, William Cobbett, Robert Browning, Edward Bulwer Lytton, William Makepeace Thackeray, and Charles Dickens that accounts for the mark it made upon the literature of the age; in the words of murder scholar Albert Borowitz, it was the most "literary" of British murders.

At length, the case was submerged in the tidal flood of crime in which the nineteenth century culminated, and its notoriety forgotten. But after the lapse of two centuries, it may be instructive—it may even, in a morbid way, be entertaining—to go back in time and see what all the fuss was about.

CHAPTER TWO

A Bad Bet

A SPORTING MAN; a *dashing* fellow; a *statute
breaker*; a Newmarket *lounger* . . .
> —*Gradus ad Cantabrigiam (1824)*

The crape-and-bombazine business, a branch of the silk trade, is apt to seem dull to anyone who has tasted a higher sort of life. So, at any rate, it seemed to Jack Thurtell, who in January 1821 was a rising young crape-and-bombazine man in the English city of Norwich. The son of a prosperous burgher, Thurtell devoted laborious days to the production of twilled and twisted silk; but he dreamt of becoming something more—he dreamt of becoming a sporting man. He was passionately fond of boxing; and already, at the age of twenty-six, he was a familiar figure in the sporting circles of London. The previous summer he had got up a fight, in a meadow in Norfolk, between Painter and Oliver, the celebrated boxers. The feat favorably impressed even the jaded connoisseurs of the capital, and in his hour of triumph Thurtell seemed to outshine the pugilists themselves. The author George Borrow, then a mere stripling, remembered how, as Thurtell drove through the twilight in a splendid barouche, his face illumined by a blood-red sky, he seemed the master of the scene, the "lord of the concourse."

For there was something in Thurtell's look and manner that enforced respect. His eyes "were grey, with an expression in which there was sternness blended with something approaching to feline." He was extraordinarily muscular, and the lower part of his face was large and powerful, like a mastiff's jowl. But it was not his looks alone, or even his bodily strength, that accounted for the ascendancy he obtained over other men. It was the union of physical prowess and a certain lightness of touch—the easy smile, the ready joke—that made Jack Thurtell lord and master of the spheres in which he moved.

At the beginning of 1821 he was in London, where his silks fetched £1,500, a great sum in those days. But the money he made from the sale was not altogether his; he owed the greater part of it to creditors in Norwich, merchants who had supplied him with the materials out of which he had fashioned his wares. They, however, could wait; the gambling clubs of Pall Mall and Spring Gardens beckoned. In them, swells in striped waistcoats and wide pantaloons sauntered about at their ease, living on their winnings from billiards or roulette, the turf or the prize-ring. For Thurtell, each was a model to be emulated.

There was old Rexworthy, in whose billiard rooms young men of fashion were daily fleeced of large sums. There was Tom "Squire" Elliot, "a gentleman of fortune, and a great patron of the prize-ring sports, the turf, &c." And there was William Weare (the last name pronounced to rhyme with "fear"), a dapper little man who was "particularly neat and clean in his person, and rather gentlemanly in his manners." Weare had no visible occupation, yet he appeared to be in the pink of prosperity. He was said to be courting a young lady in Bayswater, an heiress with £300 a year, and he was often to be seen, of an evening, in Rexworthy's, or in a club in Pall Mall, where he was known as a lucky hand at *Rouge et Noir*.*

Thurtell "flattered himself that he was a knowing, clever fellow"; and knowing and clever as he was, why should he not, like Weare and Elliot, have a goodish pile of his own? Nay, why should he not do as well as old Bill Crockford himself, the "Crœsus of the great community of gamesters, the Rothschild of the betting-ring"? Crockford, as every gamester knew, had started in life as a fishmonger near Temple Bar, and after sitting up at cards one night with Lord Thanet and Lord Granville had come away with £100,000.

There was nothing for it; Thurtell staked his newly acquired banknotes on the chance of a fortune. But unlike old Crockford, he lost his bet.

He could, of course, go back to Norwich, confess his folly, and throw himself on the mercy of his creditors. But Thurtell was not one to bend the suppliant knee. Toward the end of January, he appeared at Norwich, his face bruised and bloody. He claimed that he had been robbed, and a short time later he advertised, in one of the Norwich papers, a reward of £100 for the capture of the villains. But Thurtell's story that he had been set upon by footpads was not believed. He was declared a bankrupt and soon thereafter absconded to London.

Hell, Shelley said, is a city much like London, and, like the infernal City of Dis, the London in which Jack Thurtell sought to push his fortune had its different circles of perdition. For the aristocracy, life passed in a succession of pleasures. Glittering chariots, with coats of

---

* *Rouge et Noir* is a form of roulette in which bets are made as to which color the roulette wheel will show.

arms blazoned on the panels and powdered footmen standing on the footboards, flashed through the streets, carrying gentlefolk from one opulent house to the next. There were dinners, soirées, balls, levées, and in rooms done up in yellow satin or Genoa velvet the magnificos drank old claret and dined on pheasants stuffed with pâté de foie gras. In the intervals between parties there was Parliament, for in their spare time the grandees, "coaxed and dandled into eminence" by a nepotistic system that favored blood over brains, governed an empire that stretched from Saskatchewan to Singapore.

In their more serious hours, they made dissipation into an art, after the fashion of Byron's dying patrician, who, "having voted, dined, drunk, gamed, and whored," breathed his last and gave "the family vault another lord." The apathetic scions of pedigreed families amused themselves by drinking champagne from human skulls or losing vast sums in "deep play" at their clubs. They scattered their seed promiscuously in the bawdy houses of Soho and Covent Garden, or squandered their patrimony on the turf of Epsom and Ascot. George Payne of Sulby Hall was not yet twenty when he lost £21,000 in bets at Doncaster in September 1823. "If one could suppose such a knockdown blow wd. cure him," the society diarist Thomas Creevey wrote, "it might turn out to be money well laid out; but I fear that is hopeless."

Unlike their male counterparts, high-bred ladies could not allay their boredom with politics and prostitutes. They could not even divert themselves, as their men-folk did, by going down to Leicester Square to take in the scandalous performances in the patent theaters, which were judged too degrading to be witnessed by decent women. The lady who found herself *ennuyé* to the last degree was not, however, without resources. If she were bold, she took a lover; if vain, she amused herself with the extravagancies of dress and ornament. "Lady Londonderry is the great shew of the balls here in her jewels," Creevey wrote in September 1824, "which are out of all question the finest I ever beheld—such immense amethysts and emeralds, &c. Poor Mrs. Carnac, who had a regular *haystack* of diamonds last night, was really nothing by the side of the other. . . ."

Other ladies of the *ton*—the highest ranks of society—found an antidote to dullness in publicly shedding the last vestiges of feminine modesty. The spirit of Miss Chudleigh, who in the eighteenth century appeared at a masquerade "so naked," Horace Walpole said, "that you would have taken her for Andromeda," was alive in Regency London, and indeed attained a new height when at a dinner party Lady Caroline Lamb served up her own flesh for dessert, springing nude from a silver tureen.

Yet however outwardly splendid it was, the life of the grandees was not without its savor of horror. Lady Caroline would herself succumb to it: the romantic heroine who in a fit of mania bedded Lord Byron in the spring of 1812 died a lunatic, in 1828, at forty-two. The destiny of another Regency magnifico, Francis Charles Seymour-Conway, third Marquess of Hertford, was as black. The model for Thackeray's Lord Steyne and Disraeli's Lord Monmouth, Seymour-Conway was "a sharp, cunning, luxurious, avaricious man of the world" given up to "undisguised debauchery." One day, he went down to his villa in Richmond, a fat, swollen, grotesque figure, intent on another gaudy night with his trio of whores. He drank a glass of champagne and, looking up in terror, cried out that the devil had come for him. His valet rushed over to him and found him dead.

But however damnable the ways of the aristocrats, life in London's lower depths was more palpably hellish. Scarcely a mile from the palaces of St. James's Square were the rookeries of St. Giles, where, a contemporary wrote, "multitudes of the squalid and dissolute poor" lived, and where filth, vermin, and disease throve "with the most rank luxuriance." While Lady Caroline danced in Devonshire House and Seymour-Conway whored in Dorchester House, unwashed children frolicked in the mire of the Seven Dials, interrupting their play only to scratch the infected pustules on their scalps, or to go into gin-palaces where they stood "on tiptoe to pay for half a glass of gin." Nakedness in these quarters was not, as in Mayfair, exhibited on silver platters, or betwixt silken sheets; in Dyott Street, a notorious sink of poverty and vice where lodgings were to be had for as little as twopence, men and women, often strangers to one another, lay together in foul beds or in stalls strewn with soiled straw. One physician told a committee of the House of Commons that in such establishments he had come upon lodgers "without a single shred or piece of linen to clothe their bodies." They were "perfectly naked," or clothed only "with vermin."

CHAPTER THREE

False as Dicers' Oaths

> It is a curious feature in the career of a gambler
> at these "hells," that he gets reconciled, appar-
> ently, to his degradation and downfall: though
> now and then a thought of happier days, and
> of what he might have been, flashes across his
> mind, and penetrates his heart with a desolate
> misery.
>
> —*The London Literary Gazette (1827)*

I t was through such streets that Jack Thurtell made his way to
his own abyss. More often than not, his destination was one
or another of a class of houses in the vicinity of Piccadilly,
the Haymarket, or the "Quadrant" at the south end of Regent
Street. A handsome gas lamp illuminated the door. Going in,
he would find himself in a passage that led to another door, this

one plated with iron and covered with green or red baize—the recognized hallmark of a gaming establishment. Such places were "appropriately denominated 'hells,'" a contemporary writer said, and he believed that there were more of them in London than in any other city in the world.

The "proprietors, or more properly speaking, the bankers of these houses of robbery," according to an article in *The Westminster Review*, "are composed, for the most part, of a heterogeneous mass of worn-out gamblers, black legs,* pimps, horse-dealers, jockeys, valets, petty-fogging lawyers, low tradesmen, and have-been dealers at their own, or other houses." They preyed upon rich and poor alike, but the rich were of course the most desirable victims. William Weare, in the prospectus for his *Rouge et Noir* establishment in Pall Mall, described the house as "a Select Club, to be composed of those gentlemen only whose habits and circumstances entitle them to an uncontrolled, but proper indulgence in the amusements of the day." The grandees must indeed have laughed at the vulgarity of this; but the vulgarity was part of the fun. The larger gaming houses were gauchely fitted up "as a bait for the fortunes of the great." Invitations to dinner were "sent to noblemen and gentlemen," and those who accepted were "treated with every delicacy, and the most intoxicating wines." After dinner, a "visit to the French hazard-table in the adjoining room" was "a matter of course." A man "thus allured to the den, may determine not to lose more than the few pounds he has about him; but in the intoxication of the moment, and the delirium of play, it frequently happens that, notwithstanding the best resolves, he borrows money upon his checks, which being known to be good, are readily cashed to very considerable amounts. In this

---

* In the eighteenth century, a "black leg" was a turf swindler, but the term came later to designate other varieties of swindling rogues: more especially, the "sharper" or fraudulent gamester.

manner, £10,000, £20,000, £30,000, or more, have often been swept away."*

It was in this Hogarthian atmosphere of luxury and dissipation, of great expectations and imminent ruin, that Thurtell attempted to retrieve his fallen fortunes. At the same time, he took the lease of a public house, the Black Boy in Long Acre between Drury Lane and Covent Garden, signing the document in the name of one of his brothers. (As an absconded bankrupt, he could hardly use his own name.) Thurtell's motive in taking the Black Boy seems not to have been to make money, but rather to make a name for himself by creating a congenial resort for gaming men. He installed as barmaid one of his Norwich sweethearts, a girl with "a fine full figure" called Miss Dodson, and he was soon "hailed as a jolly good fellow" by those who came to sup with him or to drink of his "prime liquors." The refreshment was "cheap and good," one of his acquaintances remembered, and "a number of *choice spirits* in the town handled a knife and fork" at his table, or "took their glass in the evening" with him.

Thurtell soon found himself in the clutches of the rankest gamesters of the metropolis, confederates of a mysterious Mr. Lemon, one of the "cryptarchs" or secret rulers of London's gaming netherworld. These black legs, though they were outwardly all

---

* Some patricians, so far from discouraging their sons from gambling, took pains to initiate them in the costly amusement. Among these was Henry Fox, Lord Holland, who educated his boys, Lord Shelburne wrote, with an "extravagant vulgar indulgence." In the spring of 1763, Lord Holland "could think of no better diversion than to take Charles from his books, and convey him to the Continent on a round of idleness and dissipation. At Spa his amusement was to send him every night to the gaming-table with a pocketful of gold; and, (if family tradition may be trusted where it tells against family credit,) the parent took not a little pains to contrive that the boy should leave France a finished rake." Charles James Fox was fourteen years old at the time, and a scholar at Eton. On the other hand, it is said that the Duke of Wellington became a member of Crockford's only in order that he might blackball his son, Lord Douro, in the event he sought election to the club. The Duke, who thought nothing of the satire of cartoonists, admitted that there was one caricature of himself that genuinely pained him—Douro.

smiling affability, looked upon Thurtell as little more than "a good flat"—a "flatty gory," a naïf to be plundered. Behind his back they called him the "Swell Yokel" and were eager to get "a *slice* of his *blunt* (cash)."

Mr. Lemon and his minions were deeply versed in all the arts of crooked gaming, and Jack Thurtell was soon near to being bled dry by them. At last he could take no more; exasperated by his continual losses, he questioned Mr. Lemon's good faith. The prudent villain soothed his victim's rage and suspicion with a conciliatory invitation. Would Thurtell like to come down to Wadesmill, where the boxer Tom Hickman was in training? Naturally, Thurtell leapt at the chance. Hickman was the foremost pugilist of the day, ferocious "even to bull-dog fierceness," and known as the "gas-light man" because his punches "put the lights out."

CHAPTER FOUR

The Rake's Progress

flesh'd villains, bloody dogs

—Shakespeare

Wadesmill, a pleasant village on the road from London to Cambridge, stands not far from Ware, the old brewing town. Thurtell went down in the company of Miss Dodson and took rooms in the Feathers, a coaching inn still extant. It was a brilliant time. "Squire" Elliot, Hickman's principal backer, was there; so, too, was Baird, the proprietor of a hazard table in Oxenden Street. Thurtell was in his element, and he soon devised a training regimen for Hickman: "exercise and abstinence, abstinence and exercise." But after a hard day of physical exertion, a little play could do no harm, and in the evenings Thurtell took his seat at the card table.

His luck had changed for the better. Mr. Weare, whom Thurtell knew from Rexworthy's, had joined the company, as "neat and clean in his person" as ever. Whether he brought his gun and hunting dogs with him—Weare was fond of a day's shooting—has not transpired; but Thurtell was doubtless gratified to find himself beating the veteran player so regularly at Blind Hookey.

Weare affected the character of a lawyer—more precisely, of a solicitor; and he had chambers in Lyon's Inn, the nursery of such luminaries of the Bar as John Selden and Sir Edward Coke. But he was not a lawyer. A "man of low birth" and "slender education," he had started in life as a tavern waiter. Later he found a place in a gaming house, got up a thinnish veneer of gentlemanliness, and by degrees became a croupier and a leg. In addition to his *Rouge et Noir* table in Pall Mall, he had an interest in a couple of gaming houses in the East End. No spider, it was said, darted with more alacrity upon a fly than Weare upon a novice gambler. After drawing Thurtell in with an affectation of unskillfulness, he took him for £300, skinning him of his last sovereign guinea.

———•———

Thurtell's situation was now desperate. The £1,500 he had filched from his creditors was gone. The license of the Black Boy was revoked. And yet we catch a glimpse of him, in December 1821, in all his habitual swagger, riding in the Bath Mail to Newbury. At Reading a fellow passenger, who had been up on the box with the coachman, took shelter from a dripping mist in the saloon of the coach, and there made the acquaintance of Thurtell. Both men were going up for the fight between William Neate and the "gas-light man," and Thurtell expounded to his brother aficionado his philosophy of training: "exercise and abstinence, abstinence and exercise." He soon fell into a heavy slumber. But his fellow passenger did not forget him; he was William Hazlitt, and he recorded his encounter with Thurtell in his essay "The Fight."

In the summer of 1822, as Thurtell descended ever deeper into the hell of gaming, another hell-diver was exploring a different pit. Thomas De Quincey, thirty-six years old, had in his own explorations of the abyss already made notable discoveries, and the previous year that black pearl of English letters, the *Confessions of an English Opium-Eater,* had appeared in installments in the *London Magazine.* The writing had cost De Quincey great pains, and he had found himself relying on the very opium-demon he was anatomizing to see the piece through the press. But in the summer of 1822 he was trying to wean himself from his "dark idol," the opium tincture known as laudanum to which he had for many years been addicted.

De Quincey had been born in 1785, in Liverpool, the son of a prosperous merchant who died young. He was a brilliant scholar; "that boy," one of his schoolmasters said, "could harangue an Athenian mob, better than you or I could an English one." But the boy could not endure a settled routine. He ran away from school; had adventures in Wales; explored the "unfathomed" depths of London. He dissipated his fortune; studied at Oxford without taking a degree; was admitted to the society of the Lake Poets, and had become friends with its two foremost figures, Wordsworth and Coleridge. Such experiences, duly recorded in books and essays, were the foundation of De Quincey's literary reputation: so also was his opium-taking. For opium was not merely the subject of the book that made him famous: it was a literary tool, one that, if it was ruinous to his health, enabled him to illuminate those deeper levels of experience which the eighteenth-century writers had overlooked.

Perhaps, then, it was for the best that his attempt to kick the habit failed. "I must premise," De Quincey wrote a friend from his retreat at Fox Ghyll in the Lake District, "that about 170 or 180 drops [of laudanum] had been my ordinary allowance for many months. Occasionally I had run up as high as five hundred, and once nearly to 700.* In repeated preludes to my final experiment I had also gone as low as 100 drops, but had found it impossible to stand it beyond the fourth day, which, by the way, I have always found more difficult to get over than any of the preceding three."

"I went off," he said, "under easy sail—130 drops a day for three days; on the fourth I plunged . . . to 80. The misery which I now suffered 'took the conceit' out of me at once; and for about a month I continued off and on about this mark; then I sunk to 60, and the next day to—none at all. This was the first day for nearly ten years that I had existed without opium." It was agony—"*infandum dolorem,*" grief not to be uttered, though symptoms might be enumerated: "violent biliousness; rheumatic pains; then pains resembling internal rheumatism—and many other evils; but all trifles compared with the unspeakable, overwhelming, unutterable misery of mind which came on in one couple of days, and has continued almost unabatingly ever since."

As De Quincey lay, that summer, in a darkened room, "tossing and sleepless for want of opium," he amused himself "with composing the imaginary *Confessions of a Murderer,*" the "subject being," he said, "exquisitely diabolical." These murderous *Confessions* were never committed to paper, or at any rate were never delivered to the world; but the exercise bore fruit in a little essay on murder, the first of several De Quincey would write. It was to shed a curious light on what was to be the most notorious murder of the age.

———•———

In spite of so many reversals of fortune, Jack Thurtell was as sanguine as ever, and in the autumn of 1822 he even appeared to

---

* De Quincey said that at the height of his opium addiction he had taken "so large a quantity as a thousand drops" of laudanum a day.

contemplate a return to the crape-and-bombazine business. He purchased £500 worth of fabric, the money apparently furnished him by his father in Norwich; and he leased a space in Watling Street in the East End, just above a wine-and-spirits shop kept by a man named Penny. He then set about making repairs to the property. These were of a peculiar nature; and it was noted that, among other things, he instructed the carpenter to board up all the windows of the place. A short time later, he went to the offices of the County Fire Office in Regent Street. There, in a spacious office overlooking Piccadilly Circus, he insured the merchandise at Watling Street for £2,500.

Not long afterward, in January 1823, he went out on the town. He crossed Westminster Bridge into Lambeth, and in the Mitre Tavern came upon an acquaintance, Joseph Ensor, a young clerk in the Bank of England. They had a drink together, and Thurtell told Ensor he had tickets for the opera. Would Ensor care to join him? It happened that some of Ensor's family were to be at the opera that night, and the young man accepted the invitation. It was snowing when they reached Covent Garden. The opera was *Maid Marian*, the story drawn, the playbill said, "from one of Mr. Peacock's very clever novels." Afterwards, Thurtell and Ensor sauntered in the crush-room. But the crowd was great, and Ensor could see nothing of his family. It was snowing hard when he and Thurtell went out again. Ensor proposed that they go for a drink at the Cock, a tavern in the Haymarket. "No," Thurtell said, "I will take you to a better place; I will take you to the Saloon in Piccadilly."

In the Saloon they sat carousing till a late hour. The snow lay deep in Piccadilly when, at half past four, they ventured forth. "It was the most dreadful night I ever remember," Ensor said; "there was snow half up the leg."

"Let us try and get a coach," he said to Thurtell.

But there were no coaches to be had, and he and Thurtell made their way through the snow on foot. When they reached the King's Mews, where the National Gallery now stands, Thurtell said, "You had better go and take a bed at the warehouse" in Watling Street. "No," Ensor said, "I will go to my mother's." They parted. Ensor went down Whitehall, where he heard the Horse Guards' clock striking five. Thurtell went east to the Strand and reached his lodgings on Garlick Hill sometime before dawn.

The next morning, he was lying in bed with Miss Dodson when the washerwoman came in, greatly excited. Mr. Penny's shop in Watling Street was in flames.

Thurtell lounged languidly in the bed.

"Thurtell," Miss Dodson said, "the warehouse is on fire; get up, come on, get up!"

Thurtell called for the landlady and told her to grease his boots (to protect the leather against the snow). He later submitted a claim to the County Fire Office for £1,913 in losses as a result of the conflagration.

Thurtell seemed at last to have gotten the better of fortune. But Barber Beaumont, the head of the County Fire Office, was suspicious. Thurtell, he conceded, appeared to have a solid alibi, having been out all night with a Bank of England man. But curiously enough, no traces of burnt fabric were found in the ashes of Watling Street. Nor had Thurtell been able to produce the customary certification, signed by two inhabitants of the parish, that the fire was the result of accident, not arson. Beaumont refused to pay. Thurtell brought suit against him and won his case. The court awarded him £1,900. As for poor Mr. Penny, the wine-and-spirits man, he had no insurance and was ruined.

CHAPTER FIVE

The Wounded Egotist

A great deal of bankrupt vanity had taken quite
the malignant shape.

—*Thomas Carlyle*

On the surface, life was as amusing as ever. Thurtell, who was again in money, took the lease of another public house, the Cock in the Haymarket, and acquired an interest in a house in Manchester Buildings, Westminster, a stone's throw from the Thames, which was to be a repository for fraudulently obtained goods. Yet he was uneasy. All around him there were ominous portents. His brother Tom was teetering on the edge of bankruptcy; and in May his old friend Squire Elliot met his lurid end. That gentleman of fortune was awakened one morning in his house in Hunter Street, Brunswick Square, by the sheriff's officer, come to arrest him for debt. Dressed only in his nightshirt, he begged a moment's leave. Retiring to his bedroom, he sat down and put a horse pistol to his belly. The jurors at the coroner's inquest charitably returned a verdict of insanity.

A Greek chorus could not more effectually have admonished Thurtell of the fleeting nature of a sporting man's prosperity. He had long been accustomed to defy conventional prudences and restraints, and had trusted to the charm and swagger of his person to see him through. But it was not enough; charm, he now conceived, was nothing without an income; he must look about him if he were to procure a steady stream of funds.

Among the habitués of the Cock was a wine merchant named Probert. He was in his early thirties, and of a gigantic physical stature; his wine business had recently failed, with debts of £14,000. But he was not stony broke, for some years before he had married a Miss Noyes, the generously dowered daughter of a prosperous brewer whose money was beyond the reach of his creditors. Miss Noyes—she was now Mrs. Probert—had an unwed sister with dowry money of her own. Here, Thurtell thought, was the means to an income.

One day, Probert took Thurtell down to his country "lodge," a cottage near Radlett in Hertfordshire, where he introduced him to his sister-in-law. When Thurtell returned to London, he professed himself in love with the lady. The comely Miss Dodson was peremptorily dismissed; her embraces no longer pleased him; he *must* wed Miss Noyes. She, however, had promised her hand to another, a Major Woods. Thurtell determined to supplant the obnoxious rival, and whenever practicable he went down to Probert's cottage to call upon the lady. But it was in vain; a chum of Thurtell's recalled how "one Saturday, when he was going down there, he met Major Woods and Miss Noyes coming to town in company together." This "very much vexed and mortified him"; but when he endeavored to retrieve the situation by writing love letters to Miss Noyes, they "were either unnoticed or returned under cover." This "only served to irritate" Thurtell still more, and "he inveighed most bitterly against Woods."

The failure of the love-suit was followed by a still more consequential reverse. A grand jury indicted Thurtell for conspiracy to defraud Barber Beaumont's County Fire Office.* For the first time, his bright assurance failed him. An abyss had opened up before him, and he was consumed by morose thoughts. In his bedroom above the Cock, he poured forth a stream of vituperation against those who had betrayed him, punctuating the wild invectives with bullets fired from an air gun. But the Cock itself soon became too hot for him; there were warrants out against him, and he was liable to arrest at any moment. Probert advised him to take refuge in the Coach and Horses, an inn on Conduit Street. Mr. Tetsall, the proprietor, was an obliging fellow and would "keep a good lookout" for him.

At the Coach and Horses, the wounded egotist wallowed in his grievances. He dreamt of revenge. Major Woods was to be the first victim. Thurtell would invent some spurious pretext to entice him to come to the warehouse in Manchester Buildings, where he would bludgeon him to death with a pair of dumbbells. One of his confederates, a slow-witted fellow named Joe Hunt, promised to assist him in the business.

Dressed as a servant, Hunt went one morning to Major Woods's lodgings in Castle Street and told him that Mrs. Brew (a great friend of Woods's) wished him to come at once to a house in Westminster. Major Woods followed Hunt to 10 Manchester Buildings. The door was ajar, and Hunt went in, expecting Woods to follow. But when he looked round, he saw that Woods had stopped on the threshold, being "no doubt deterred from going in" by the sight of Thurtell standing "at the foot of the stairs, close to the back parlour door, with his coat and shoes off, a red shawl over his head to disguise him, and a dumb bell in each hand ready to strike."

---

* The jury was satisfied that before the fire in Watling Street, Thurtell had sold the fabrics he had insured to two purchasers, William Steadman, a merchant in Cumberland Street, and the firm of Margrave & Co. His actual losses in the fire did not exceed a hundred pounds.

Deterred Major Woods no doubt was, and a moment later was seen judiciously running off.

"It was lucky for him he did run," Thurtell said, "or else he would never have run again." He toyed with other plans for doing away with Major Woods, but in the meantime his cronies were becoming impatient. "Damn and blast Woods," one of them exclaimed. "What is the use of killing him? Barber Beaumont is the man we want out of the way." "Never fear," Thurtell replied: "he is booked . . . you may depend on it." And indeed, for several nights Thurtell lay in wait for Beaumont with his air gun. But Beaumont, too, eluded him.

CHAPTER SIX

Ultra Flash Men

Weare, Thurtell, Hunt, and Probert, were all
sporting blades, ultra *flash men*, and gamblers—
preying alike upon each other. . . .
　　　　　—*The Fatal Effects of Gambling (1824)*

The maples were beginning to change color when, on an afternoon in October 1823, Jack Thurtell and his brother Tom were walking in Spring Gardens, near the eastern end of St. James's Park. With them was Joe Hunt. As they approached Rexworthy's billiard rooms, Jack expressed a desire to go in. He exchanged a few words with Rexworthy himself, then went over to a fastidiously dressed little man who was sitting at one of the tables.

"Mr. Weare, how are you?"

Weare stood up and shook hands. After an interchange of pleasantries, the two men left the room together. When, some twenty minutes later, they returned, Tom Thurtell said he must be off. Jack, too, had to be going, and he and Hunt went out together. Hunt would later recall how, as they went up the Haymarket, Jack told him how he had accused Weare of cheating him with false cards. "You dare not say a word," Weare had replied, "for you know you have defrauded your creditors of that money"; and he had afterwards refused Thurtell a loan of five pounds. "Go and rob for it as I do," he told the desperate supplicant.

"I do not forget this treatment," Thurtell said.

——•——

While Thurtell struggled in the pit, another young man, a year his junior, was beginning his ascent from the regions of the damned. In October 1823, Thomas Carlyle was living in Kinnaird House in the Tay Valley of Scotland, having sequestered himself to "clean and purify" himself in the "penal fire" of his own inward inferno. It was (he supposed) the price of illumination. As his fellow mystic and somewhatish friend De Quincey said, "Either the human being must suffer and struggle as the price of a more searching vision, or his gaze must be shallow, and without intellectual revelation." After a tussle in the pit "with the foul and vile and soul-murdering Mud-Gods" of his epoch, Carlyle took up the prophetic mantle and howled, much as Isaiah and Jeremiah had howled before him. The customs of his people were vain: fed on a diet of materialism and rationalism, they were withered up, he said, "into effete Prose, dead as ashes." Having sacrificed the native splendor of their being on the altars of profit and loss, they were become automatized, pattern-figure persons, unacquainted with the "mystic deeps" of their souls. They had sold their birthright for a mess of merchandise, and were less content than ever.

It was, Carlyle said, characteristic of his generation that it should crave romance, yet fail to see that romance was all around them. Even in an age of prose and political economy, there were romantic passions great enough to "suspend men from bed-posts" and "from improved-drops at the west end of Newgate" prison. A passion that "explosively shivers asunder the Life it took rise in," he wrote, "ought to be regarded as considerable; no more passion, in the highest heyday of Romance, yet did. The passions, by grace of the Supernal and also of the Infernal Powers (for both have a hand in it), can never fail us." Yet Carlyle's own passional architecture was warped. His words and thoughts were as iron, but his man-hood was soft, flaccid—limp. As he lay amid the doleful shades of Kinnaird House, he was courting, through the post, Jane Baillie Welsh, whom he was later to marry. The marriage would never be consummated, and the passion that found no healthy outlet became muckish and unclean, like the waters of a standing pond. Ever thrifty, Carlyle converted his thwarted passion into the prose with which he made his name and reputation. Time has since tarnished his fame as an Eminent Victorian; but for the historian of murder he will always have his value. The morose star-voyaging philoso-pher, angrily condemning the "dim millions mostly blockhead" whom he simultaneously sought to enlighten, was able to cut to the core of a lowly, flesh-and-blood crime more readily than those who, as Lord Byron said of himself, had no "poetical humbug" in them and piqued themselves on their practicality. There was "endless mystery," Carlyle said, in even the crudest *fact*, a "Sentence printed if not by God, then at least by the Devil," a "hieroglyphic page" in which one could "read on forever, find new meaning forever." Of all those who were soon to interest themselves in the facts of Jack Thurtell's murderous career, few would see farther into their significance than Thomas Carlyle.

———•———

In the middle of October, Thurtell went again to Rexworthy's and spoke affably to Weare. Rexworthy afterwards heard from Weare himself an account of the conversation and supposed that the two men were reconciled. So far from nursing a grudge against his old antagonist, Thurtell had invited him to come down to Hertfordshire with him for few days' shooting. Weare had accepted the invitation.

Not long afterwards, Thurtell came across Hunt in the Coach and Horses. "Hunt," he said, "I wish you would take a walk with me."

It was a brisk fall day, the mercury reaching fifty-six. The two men, the one tall and commanding, the other short and sullen-faced, went up to Oxford Street together and crossed into Marylebone, where they stopped before the window of a jeweler's shop. Thurtell was intrigued by a pair of pistols on display. They went in, and Thurtell told the shop-man he wanted to kill some cats. He purchased both guns.

When Thurtell and Hunt returned to the Coach and Horses, Probert was there. He chided Thurtell for his failure to "book" Major Woods. "You made a bad business of that, Jack," he said, adding that he doubted whether an air gun could kill a man "on the spot."

Thurtell brandished his newly acquired pistols. "I know that as well as you, Bill, or what the hell should I buy these pops for? I was a bloody fool to go all the way to my friend Harper, at Norwich, to borrow the air gun."

They melted the lead to make the balls and cast four bullets.

Probert said he doubted whether the balls were large enough to kill a man "on the spot."

"You would be damned sorry to have one of them through your head, small as they are," Thurtell replied.

The pistols were loaded, and Hunt greased the hammers and the triggers.

"Bill," he said to Probert, "will you be in it?"

CHAPTER SEVEN

Lyon's Inn

But I full of thoughts and trouble touching the
issue of this day; and to comfort myself did go to
the Dog and drink half-a-pint of mulled sack. . . .
—*Samuel Pepys*

Turning out of the Strand, you went down Holywell Street
past crooked houses with weirdly carven gables and book-
venders who did a brisk trade in disreputable literature.
The shops of Holywell Street were notorious for the variety of
publications on offer, but respectable material was also to be had.
If you happened to be browsing in October 1823, your eye might
perhaps have fallen on the most recent issue of the *London Magazine*, just come from the press. The lead article, "Notes from the
Pocket-Book of a Late Opium-Eater," was by Thomas De Quincey
and contained the first of his published meditations on murder,
"On the Knocking at the Gate in *Macbeth*."

Continuing down Holywell Street, you were soon before the Old Dog Tavern, where Samuel Pepys used now and again to have his "liquor up." Nearby was a passage that led to Lyon's Inn. Passing through the portal, you found yourself in a gloomy court. "A more silent, haunted-looking inn was never known," an old lawyer remembered. "Even by daylight, strange shadows flitted about the dwarfish doorways, and fled up the spiral staircases into the low-pitched upper stories."

In the reign of Queen Elizabeth, Sir Edward Coke held the office of Reader here, astonishing or more likely boring his auditors with his intricate expositions of the common and the statutory law. But in the autumn of 1823, Lyon's Inn was the most disreputable of the Inns of Chancery, those ancient seminaries of English equity practice. It was now inhabited by doubtful characters, mountebanks and fraudsters, as well as by unsavory attorneys, the "vermin of the law"—an ironic reversal, in light of the tradition that those who seek "equity must come with clean hands." Lyon's Inn reeked of decay; yet on this particular afternoon, William Weare, in his chambers in the southeast corner, was in high spirits. He was looking forward to a few days' shooting in Hertfordshire, and to practicing the still more agreeable sport of "flat-catching" there. He was, no doubt, pleased that Jack Thurtell had come round, and was eager to cooperate with him in the netting of an unsuspecting naïf. Just the other day, Thurtell had come over to Rexworthy's to let him know that he had recently become acquainted with a young gentleman who had come into a large property in Hertfordshire. Thurtell particularly mentioned that the young man had a passion for gaming yet refused to play for small stakes. What was more, the opulent youth had invited him to come down to his country house for some shooting, and had no objection to his bringing a friend.

Thurtell had evidently learned his lesson: he spoke of introducing "cards, hazard, or backgammon" after dinner in Hertfordshire, and of making a "famous thing of it." Weare was himself enchanted by the prospect and perhaps thought it to Thurtell's credit that, eager as the novice was to "decoy a flat," he yet had sense enough to turn to a master player to show him how the thing was done.

Miss Malone, the laundress, came in and laid out Weare's clothes and linen. Weare himself took out a carpetbag and began to pack it. Five shirts, six pairs of stockings, a shooting jacket, leggings, breeches, a pair of laced boots, and a pair of Wellingtons were put in, together with a razor and strop, a tortoiseshell comb and hairbrush, a backgammon board, a pair of loaded dice, and two or three packs of false cards.

Weare told Miss Malone not to bother about his supper; he was going out of town that afternoon and would not return until Tuesday. About three o'clock, he asked her to fetch a coach for him. She went over to the Spotted Dog in the Strand, and a short time later the coach rolled around to Lyon's Inn. Weare came down, slight of figure in an olive-colored coat; a gold watch hung from a chain around his neck. He put his gun into the coach before getting in himself; the girl put the carpetbag in and watched him drive off.

CHAPTER EIGHT

Young Men from the Provinces

> Fixity of tradition, of custom, of language is perhaps a prerequisite to complete harmony in life and mind. Variety in these matters is a lesson to the philosopher and drives him into the cold arms of reason; but it confuses the poet and the saint, and embitters society.
>
> —*Santayana*

H ave you got every thing you want, Jack?" Probert asked. It was past three o'clock, and Thurtell and his chums were dining together in the Coach and Horses.*

"No," Thurtell said, "we must send Joe for a six-bushel sack, a hank of cord, and the horse and chaise." He then turned to Hunt,

---

* Dinner in those days was a midday or early-afternoonish meal; the last meal of the day was supper.

and told him to fetch, too, his red shawl from the Cock, where he had inadvertently left it. He took out his pocketbook and gave Hunt some money, saying that he was specially to remember to tell the hostler that he needed the gig on account of a visit he was making to Dartford.

———•———

The coach came round to Charing Cross. Weare instructed the coachman to wait while he went over to Rexworthy's. He found Rexworthy there and told him that he was on his way to meet Thurtell at Cumberland Gate, whence they were to start together for Hertfordshire.

———•———

Just before five o'clock, Hunt drove up Conduit Street in the rented gig. It was dark-green in color; a roan-gray horse stood in the harness. The horse's cheeks were very white.

Hunt showed his mates the sack.

"I am sure this is not a six-bushel sack," Probert said. "This will not be large enough for him, Jack."

"Never mind, Bill, we must make a shift with it; we have no time to lose."

Thurtell went out to the gig and drove off. Probert and Hunt remained. Sometime before six o'clock, Probert asked Tetsall's boy to bring round his own horse and chaise. He then excused himself.

"Hunt," he said when he came back into the room, "the chaise is ready."

———•———

The coach rolled down Cumberland Street, stopping not far from where the Marble Arch now stands and where the Tyburn gallows once stood. Weare got out and went up the street toward Tyburn Turnpike, at the western end of Oxford Street. A moment later, he returned with a tall man in a rough coat. Weare paid the fare and, having collected his gun and carpetbag, went away with the man in the rough coat. It was half past four, and some of the lamps were lighted, but others were not, for the day was not yet gone.

———•———

Probert and Hunt were driving up Oxford Street when Probert said they must get something for supper; he was not sure whether there was anything to eat in the lodge. They stopped at a butcher's, and Hunt bought a loin of pork. They set off again, going down Oxford Street toward Tyburn Turnpike and passing thence into the Edgware Road. Commanding a strong bay horse, they soon overtook Thurtell and Weare.

"Here they are," Hunt said. "Drive by and take no notice."

They drove on through the darkness, the road before them faintly illuminated by the glowing oil of the gig-lamps. Probert was apprehensive. What, he asked Hunt, if Jack should "well it"—take the greatest part of the money for himself? For it was universally believed, in the gaming circles of London, that Weare never carried less than £1,000 or £1,500 on his person, a sum he kept close to his skin, ready to be instantly retrieved should an opportunity present itself.

"We know Jack is a very determined fellow," Probert said, "and is sure to do the trick; but if he don't do the thing that is right by giving us our share, we shall be sure to learn by the newspapers what amount he takes, and we shall know how to act hereafter."

Sometime before eight o'clock, they reached Elstree and stopped at the Artichoke. Mr. Field, the publican, brought them glasses of brandy-and-water, which they drank in the gig. Probert was merry and told Mr. Field that Hunt could "sing a good song."

"I should be glad to hear him," Mr. Field said.

35

But Hunt declined to sing.

Each was drinking his fourth or fifth glass of brandy-and-water when, upon hearing the sound of a horse and chaise, they sped off. As they drew near to Mr. Phillimore's lodge, about a mile from Radlett, they stopped by the side of the road.

"You get out here," Probert told Hunt. "I will go on to the cottage, and see if Jack is there, and if he is all right."

———•———

An officer of the Bow Street Horse Patrol, in a blue coat and scarlet waistcoat, was riding near the fifth milestone in the Edgware Road when he saw two men driving hard in a gig drawn by a roan-gray horse with a white face. A little later a man named Clarke, landlord of the White Lion in Edgware, was going up the road on foot when, turning round, he saw a gig bearing down on him at a furious rate. The driver shouted at him to get out of the way. Clarke recognized him; it was Jack Thurtell, a man who had often raised a glass in the White Lion.

The roads around London had long been the scene of robbery and violence. The better to keep the King's Peace on the frontiers of the metropolis, the mounted officers of the Patrol had been commissioned to supplement the efforts of "Mr. Fielding's People," the Bow Street Runners, who were on foot.* Partly as a result of the Patrol, the great age of highway robbery had come to an end. But the names of the highwaymen who once haunted the desolate heaths lived on, not least in the imaginations of young miscreants who sought to emulate such villains as Richard "Dick" Turpin and John "Sixteen-String Jack" Rann.

---

* During the first half of the eighteenth century, London had no regular police force. In December 1748, Henry Fielding, the author of *Tom Jones*, became Magistrate and Justice of the Peace for the county of Middlesex and the City and Liberties of Westminster; and he soon thereafter recruited a number of constables to assist him in the detection of criminals.

Thurtell himself traded jests with Hunt about their being "Turpins" and "Turpin lads." Like Turpin, who had been born, in 1705, near Saffron Walden in Essex, Thurtell, too, was a young man from the provinces: he had forsaken his provincial Norwich to make his fortune in London. Such transplantations were one of the great social facts of the age. With the consolidation of the nation states which in the sixteenth and seventeenth centuries replaced the more loosely organized kingdoms of Christendom, cities like London and Paris acquired an ever-greater importance. Provincial towns like Dijon and Prague, Aix and Salamanca, with their high proud traditions, suffered a corresponding decline. The provinces, Honoré de Balzac wrote in one of his novels, became as stale as stagnant water.

The metropolises of Europe—and none more so than London—became a magnet for young men seduced by tales of the riches that were (in theory) to be easily won there. The adventures of the most gifted of these young men have been told, not only by Balzac himself, but by Stendhal and Flaubert, Henry James and Lionel Trilling. These writers were, not unnaturally, drawn to the highest specimens of the type, which they brought to life in such characters as Hyacinth Robinson, the hero of James's *The Princess Casamassima*, and Julien Sorel, the hero of Stendhal's *Le Rouge et le Noir*. They had no desire to chronicle the misdeeds of young provincials molded out of coarser stuff: *their* histories were left to the journeymen of letters, to the Grub Street hacks whose lives of the ne'er-do-wells fill the pages of the *Newgate Calendar*, that dark companion-volume and obverse mirror of the *Lives of the Saints*.

No one would mistake Jack Thurtell for Balzac's Lucien de Rubempré or James's Hyacinth Robinson: he had nothing of their delicate idealism, their instinct for form, or their personal beauty. And yet Thurtell was, in his own way, quite as much a provincial ingénu as either of them: and his own metropolitan pilgrimage was to come to quite as dark an end.

———•———

A little before eight o'clock, a laborer was coming out of a field near Gill's Hill Lane, the road beside which Probert's cottage stood. The moon was not yet up: there was only starlight. In the dimness, he saw a gig come down the lane. There were two men in it.

———•———

Had Jack Thurtell chanced to have been born in an earlier age, he might never have felt the lure of London. Under different stars, he might have been content to have remained a Norwich man, for the city in its prime was one of the sweetest of provincial nectaries. It is difficult for us today to form a just conception, not merely of the beauty, but of the vitality of the old provincial towns as they were in the days before the West was metropolized and all eyes became engrossed in the drama of the megalopolis. "A charming and sometimes forgotten feature of the world as it used to be," Lytton Strachey wrote in his essay on Voltaire and the Président de Brosses, "was the provincial capital. When Edinburgh was as far from London as Vienna is today, it was natural—it was inevitable—that it should be the centre of a local civilization, which, while it remained politically and linguistically British, developed a colour and a character of its own. In France there was the same pleasant phenomenon. Bordeaux, Toulouse, Aix-en-Provence—up to the end of the eighteenth century each of these was in truth a capital, where a peculiar culture had grown up that was at once French and idiosyncratic. An impossibility today!" Norwich, too, had once been such a provincial center, with its own distinct and creative culture; and although in Thurtell's time it was but a pale shadow of its former self, it retained enough of its old enchantment to draw from George Borrow, in his novel *Lavengro*, a memorable tribute to its faded beauty. But Thurtell, who had taught young Borrow to box, was not such a sentimentalist as his pupil; he wanted action, and it was in London, not Norwich, that action was to be had.

Balzac in his novels invariably makes the story of the young man from the provinces into a melodrama: it is obvious from the start that the ingénu will be corrupted by the metropolis whose prizes he covets. But Balzac had got hold of a real problem: the fact is that the ingénu very often *was* corrupted by the metropolis. The life he knew in his hometown was on a human scale: everyone knew everyone else. In *Lost Illusions*, Balzac describes how, in provincial Angoulême, even those who despised Lucien de Rubempré "took him for a human being." In Paris, by contrast, the young man found that he "did not even exist" in the eyes of those among whom he was obliged to make his way. The lesson was clear, and Vautrin, the demonic figure who initiates Lucien in the corrupting arts of the capital, was quick to draw it: one must, he said, "look upon men, and women particularly, as mere tools, but without letting them realize it." It was a lesson Thurtell himself had by this time learned all too well.

—•—

The moon rose, and the trees and hedgerows showed white in the moonshine. A farmer named Smith was going with his wife and children to Battlers Green, the farm of his friend Mr. Nicholls. Smith himself was on foot; his wife and children were in an ass chaise. Their road ran roughly parallel to Gill's Hill Lane, which lay a few hundred yards to the east. About a quarter past eight, Smith was startled by the report of a pistol. "I then heard groans which lasted a minute or two." He did not, however, investigate. "I had my wife and children with me; I did not go up because my wife was alarmed."

CHAPTER NINE

Gig-Men

Sure some malignant planet
Rules o'er this night.

—Tailor

Young Tom Carlyle knew as much as Balzac or Flaubert of the ways in which the young provincial, threading his way through the labyrinths of the metropolis, is gradually demoralized. The son of a mason in Ecclefechan, in Scotland's southern uplands, Carlyle was himself a young man from the provinces. His genius had early discovered itself, and those who took an interest in his prospects were continually urging him to go to London, in much the way Madame de Bargeton, in *Lost Illusions*, urges Lucien de Rubempré to go to Paris, "the capital of the intellectual world," the stage on which the young man was sure to find success. "You must leap quickly over the gap which separates you from it," she tells him. "Don't let your ideas grow rancid in the provinces. . . . Neither distinction nor high position go looking for talent wilting away in a small town."

Two days before the Friday afternoon on which Thurtell and Weare set out for Hertfordshire, Carlyle, in a letter to Jane Baillie Welsh, told her how their mutual friend, the preacher Edward Irving, had implored him to go up to London. "He seemed to think," Carlyle wrote, "that if set down on London streets some strange development of genius would take place in me, that by conversing with Coleridge and the Opium-eater, I should find out new channels of speculation, and soon learn to speak with tongues. There is but very small degree of truth in all this."

The Calvinist in Carlyle sniffed danger in London, which figured to him as "a loud, roaring, big, pretentious, and intrinsically barren sphere" in which good men lost their way. His friend Irving was already resident there, basking in the sunshine of a brilliant but soon-to-be-eclipsed metropolitan celebrity. Irving had won fame as a pulpit orator and was much petted by society ladies and "right honourable" gentlemen. But the novelty of his preaching soon faded, and his fall from favor was followed, in short order, by disintegration and an early grave.

A common enough fate: young men from the provinces regularly went to the devil. Carlyle found the root of the problem to be the particular kind of honor to which the young men aspired— "respectability." Whatever the outward form of the young man's aspiration, inwardly he wanted to be a gentleman. Irving himself, with all his Christian idealism, was not free of the demon. He was delighted when, in the first flush of London popularity, the most respectable characters in the kingdom came to hear him preach; and he was cast down when, at length, they tired of him and sought a new trifle with which to beguile their boredom. There was, Carlyle saw, a double tragedy in such a fate. The gentlemanly ideal to which the provincial ingénu aspired was, in the nineteenth century, mostly sham-hollow, the relic of a feudalism that had long since lost its *raison d'être*. The medieval gentleman was exempted from work because he was obliged to fight; the modern gentleman accepted the leisure without the obligation to risk his life for it. The gentlemen of old, the Victorian moralist John Ruskin wrote, "not only did more, but in proportion to their doings, *got* less than other people," whereas today "superior persons" generally did less and got more than anyone else. In seeking to join the ranks of the respectable, the young man from the provinces was selling his soul for a thing essentially empty, the vacuous life of the gilded layabout. But even if the coveted thing had been really substantial, the young man could not, Carlyle saw, have attained it, for he had been bred to a different tradition, was not to the manner born. For however fastidiously a man like Thurtell aped the fashions of gentlemen, he never became a gentleman himself: at most, he became a burlesque of one.

Carlyle had not yet found an image that exactly conveyed both the pathos and the folly of the pseudo-gentility which his contemporaries craved, but Thurtell himself would soon supply him with one. "What sort of person was Mr. Weare?" asked the lawyer for the Crown at Thurtell's trial. "*Answer.* Mr. Weare was respectable. *Counsel.* What do you mean by respectability? *Witness.* He kept a gig."

Carlyle had his image. The corrupted provincial became not a gentleman but a gig-man, who rode about in a fashionable two-wheeled chaise, a Tilbury, perhaps, or a Stanhope. "The gig of respectability again!" Carlyle would exclaim to himself whenever he encountered some vulgar, gaudy, or otherwise barren form of pretension.

There was a glow of candlelight in the cottage window. The boy Addis, "servant to Mr. Probert," was at his post in the stable. Earlier in the evening, he had heard the wheels of a gig going past the cottage. He had thought it his master, but the gig had passed on.

Now someone was ringing the bell at the gate. Who in the name of Beelzebub was there?

A face the boy knew well—Mr. Thurtell's.

He was standing, in a drab-colored greatcoat, much stained, beside a horse and gig.

When Probert and Hunt reached the cottage, they went with Thurtell into the parlor. Mrs. Probert, who was just then coming down the stairs, was surprised to find a stranger among the company.

"This is my friend Hunt," Probert said to her, "of whom you have so often heard me speak as being so good a singer."

The men drank brandy, and Probert proposed that while supper was getting ready—Susan the cook was dressing the pork—he and his guests should go to Battlers Green, to ask a day's shooting of his landlord, Mr. Nicholls. They went out to the stable, where Thurtell produced Weare's gold watch and chain.

"Now I'll take you down to where he lies."

———•———

If Carlyle illuminated the gig-pretension of Thurtell, De Quincey elucidated the deeper horror of his crime. The small, delicate man, with his courteous manners and soft, enchanting voice, was a curious bearer of the dark insights which were his specialty in trade; he seemed, at first sight, to be angelically innocent. He was "hardly above five feet," Carlyle said, and "you would have taken him, by candlelight, for the beautifullest little child," had there not "been a something, too, which said, '*Eccovi*—this child has been in hell.'" *

It was true: the sensitive, retiring creature had been in hell. In his *Confessions of an English Opium-Eater*, he described the

———

* Carlyle alluded to an anecdote told of Dante: how in the streets of Verona he was pointed out with the words *"Eccovi l' uom ch' e stàto all' inferno."* ("See, there is the man that was in hell.")

horror of his drug-laden dreams. He was transported into lands of "vertical sunlight," and suffered "mythological tortures" at the hands of unscrupulous priests. He ran into pagodas and was imprisoned in their secret chambers, or fixed upon their summits. He was the idol: he was the priest: he was worshipped: he was sacrificed. Yet If De Quincey was fascinated by experiences which, like opium nightmares and metropolitan murders, had the mark of the beast upon them, he was no less drawn to the aftermaths of these experiences, when life resumed its customary aspect. He recounted how, during an opium dream in which he was being pursued by a malignant crocodile, he suddenly awoke to the pure sunshine of the English day. It "was broad noon, and my children were standing, hand in hand, at my bedside, come to show me their coloured shoes, or new frocks, or to let me see them dressed for going out." So awful, he said, was "the transition from the damned crocodile, and the other unutterable monsters and abortions of my dreams, to the sight of innocent *human* natures and of infancy, that, in the mighty and sudden revulsion of mind, I wept, and could not forbear it, as I kissed their faces." Such experiences played a part in shaping a hell-scholarship unsurpassed of its kind, one which remains even now an indispensable guide to the malefactions of Thurtell.

———•———

There was a chill in the air as the three men went down Gill's Hill Lane in the moonlight; the mercury that night would fall into the thirties.

"It is just by the second turning," Thurtell said.

They came to a spot where there was a gap in the hedge.

"This is the place."

A maple grew nearby, and Thurtell, who had lost both his pistol and his penknife in the struggle, kicked the fallen leaves in an effort to recover them.

The body lay on the other side of the hedge. Hunt held the lantern, and Probert took up the corpse by the pits of the arms. Thurtell rifled the pockets, in which he found—not much: a couple of fivers, folded carelessly together, a memorandum book, and some coins—mere silver, with no alloy of gold in them.*

"This is all he has got," Thurtell said.

They put the body into the sack, head first; but the sack was too small, and at the open end the feet stuck out.

They left the body there; and on the way back to the cottage Thurtell spoke. "As we were going along the dark lane Weare said to me, 'Damn my eyes, Jack, here's a pretty place to cut a man's throat, if you want to get rid of him!' Presently I said to him, 'I have missed the lodge gates—I must have passed them.' Then I turned the horse about, and followed your advice, Probert, by telling him how nice the country looked that way; this induced him to turn in the direction I pointed, and I shot him through the head. . . ."

But Weare had obstinately refused to die.

"I never had so much trouble to kill a man in all my life."** For "after I had discharged my pistol at him he jumped out of the gig and run." He ran "like the devil up the lane, singing out that he would deliver all he had won of me, if I would only spare his life. . . . I jumped out of the gig, and ran after him."

He "fought with me till I knocked him down with the pistol, and he then struggled with me with great resolution, and actually got me undermost. While, however, I was in this situation, I took

---

* Silver coins (crowns, half-crowns, florins, shillings, and pennies) were sharply distinguished from the guineas (sovereign guineas, half-sovereign guineas, and half-guineas), machine-struck gold coins minted in the United Kingdom as late as 1814. Neither the gold nor the silver in any of the coins was wholly pure: the guineas were said to be eleven-twelfths pure gold, and the silver coins thirty-seven parts pure silver and three parts alloy.

** Thurtell would later deny that this was true: "Weare was a very little man; and to think it possible that such a person could get the better of me, is all nonsense."

out my penknife and cut his throat, and in so doing I broke the blade of my knife. The blood rushed from him in quantities, and some got down my throat and nearly choked me: at last when his strength failed him by the loss of blood, I got up." But although Weare's throat was cut "about the jugular vein," the wound did "not stop his singing out." Thurtell then "jammed the pistol" into Weare's head. "I saw him turn round; then I knew I had done him. Joe, you ought to have been with me. . . . Those damned pistols are like spits; they are of no use."

CHAPTER TEN

The Party in the Parlor

this sore night
hath trifled former knowings.

—*Shakespeare*

I n the parlor the three men drank brandy and supped on pork. Thurtell himself, "hot from slaughtering," had no appetite and complained of feeling unwell. After dinner, Probert went into the kitchen for a bottle of rum, and Thurtell, in the good humor that comes of a warm liver, drew Weare's watch and chain from his waistcoat pocket. He urged Probert to put the chain around Mrs. Probert's neck; but this Probert declined to do. Thurtell then contrived an elaborate fiction, telling Mrs. Probert that the chain had once belonged to "a little Quakeress, a sweetheart of mine at

Norwich." But "as I have turned her up," he said, "I must beg of you to keep it for my sake."[*]

Mrs. Probert at first refused the gift, saying that it would be awkward for Mr. Thurtell to have a watch without a chain. But Thurtell persisted, and at last she allowed him to draw the chain around her neck. She received it, Hunt remembered, "very cordially," and "promised never to part with it."

The incident would shock England almost as much as the murder itself. That the man whose hands had shortly before done such bloody work should now put them, insinuatingly, caressingly, around the neck of his friend's wife, a woman whose sister he had once professed to love, a woman who was herself to come to a ghastly end—it savored, in its mixture of malignant eroticism and heartless frivolity, of a depravity foreign to the English character, or so Englishmen liked to suppose.

Having enchained Mrs. Probert, Thurtell was careful to pop the watch itself back into his pocket. But the revels were not yet ended. "You think me a good singer, Betsy," Probert said to his wife, "but you must hear my friend Mr. Hunt." Hunt was, indeed, reluctant to sing; but the company pressed him to "tip them a stave," and he acquiesced.

———————

The weird levity of the party in the parlor was for De Quincey the illustration of a psychological fact. In his essay "On the Knocking at the Gate in *Macbeth*," he explained that episodes of intense horror are commonly followed by restorations of ordinary life that reveal, as nothing else, the true blackness of what went before. Like Viking princes after the slaughter-hell of battle, embracing drink

---

[*] Thurtell said that he had once been "upon terms of intimacy with a Quaker's family at Norwich," and had privately paid his addresses to the daughter. The Quaker, however, was informed that his daughter's suitor "was a profligate bad character" and forbade him the house.

and woman-flesh with ecstatic vehemence, or sailors on leave indulging themselves in a mad carouse, the evil-doers embrace their freshly recovered normality with an insane avidity. As, during the Black Death, men and women were roused, in their revulsion from the universal horror, to a frenzied love of life, copulating promiscuously in the very cemeteries in which they were soon to be laid as corpses, so Thurtell's struggle in the death-vortex with Weare produced the voluptuous euphoria of the party in Probert's parlor.

It was a commonplace of Romantic thought that life is a marriage of heaven and hell; but De Quincey perhaps more accurately conceived it to be a cycle in which ordinary time is routinely punctuated by intervals of hellishness and intervals of grace. The cycle was for him an immutable law, yet he recognized that it manifests itself differently in different persons. A certain kind of soul embraces hellish experience, seeks it out, in the pursuit of sensuous ecstasy; another sort accepts suffering as an inevitable part of life which, when gone through, brings one closer to grace. For readers of English poetry, Hamlet is the exemplar of the soul which finds its way through suffering to peace. Having passed through an interval of moral horror, he again sees the stars:

> *There's a divinity that shapes our ends,*
> *Rough-hew them how we will. . . .*

Macbeth, on the other hand, is the pattern-figure of the soul that undertakes a hellish act in order to indulge a sensual felicity, in his case the wielding of a royal scepter. Having "done the deed" and murdered Duncan, he ascends from the world of the dead to that of the living, an ascension Shakespeare signalizes by the knocking at the gate of the castle at Glamis:

> *Whence is that knocking?*
> *How is't with me, when every noise appalls me?*

Eventually the clownish porter, who laughingly identifies himself with the "porter of hell-gate," gets up and with a stream of humorous talk opens the castle gate to admit Lenox and Macduff, and with them the breath of fresh life.

De Quincey traces the power of the scene to Shakespeare's comprehension of what murder ultimately is, an eruption of hell in the fabric of regular existence. The "world of ordinary life," he writes, is during the course of a murder "arrested, laid asleep, tranced, racked into a dread armistice." Its place is taken by a hellish world, a "world of devils," cut off by "an immeasurable gulf from the ordinary tide and succession of human affairs—locked up and sequestered in some deep recess" of perdition. The murderer himself is "conformed to the image of devils"; and a "fiendish heart" takes the place of his human one. But at length the hellishness recedes, and like the blue sky that succeeds a storm, existence resumes its wonted aspect:

> Hence it is, that when the deed is done, when the work of darkness is perfect, then the world of darkness passes away like a pageantry in the clouds: the knocking at the gate is heard; and it makes known audibly that the reaction has commenced: the human has made its reflux upon the fiendish; the pulses of life are beginning to beat again. . . .

The party in Probert's parlor has roughly the same significance, in the tragedy of Thurtell, that the knocking at the gate has in the tragedy of Macbeth. Having re-entered ordinary life, Macbeth seeks pleasure in a "great feast," much as Thurtell and his henchmen seek it in a little one. "Come, love and health to all," Macbeth cries:

> *Give me some wine; fill full.*
> *I drink to th' general joy o' th' whole table.*

Only Macbeth deviates from the familiar pattern in feeling scarcely, or not at all, the fleeting euphoria that Thurtell and his chums feel—the "Dionysian dowry," the life-enhancing intoxication, which Nietzsche says is characteristic of the feast that follows the sacrifice and productive of that "horrible mixture of sensuality and cruelty" which is the "real 'witches' brew.'"

But the euphoria is temporary, and ultimately the "re-establishment of the goings-on of the world in which we live," De Quincey says, makes the evil-doers more "profoundly sensible of the awful parenthesis that had suspended them." Macbeth, after killing Duncan, discovers that life has lost its savor; Thurtell, after killing Weare, is rapidly overtaken by despair. Macbeth no longer relishes an existence that has "fallen into the sere"—its autumnal decay; and Thurtell and his mates discover, after the first narcosis of pleasure has worn off, that grog has ceased to cheer and song to make merry. They, too, "have supp'd full with horrors," and, like Macbeth, are

cabin'd, cribb'd, confin'd, bound in
To saucy doubts and fears. . . .

CHAPTER ELEVEN

A Devil's Grammar of Debauchery

the wakeful Bird
Sings darkling

—*Milton*

A t midnight, Mrs. Probert rose from the table; her husband, however, called for another bottle of rum.

"I suppose you will make a drunken bout of it," she said to him. "I shan't disturb you."

"Yes," Thurtell said, "you may expect to see your Billy come up to bed drunk enough."

Mrs. Probert went upstairs.

"We may as well look and see if there is any *chaunt* [marking] about the money," Thurtell said. They examined Weare's five-pound notes and found no marks. Thurtell then took out Weare's note-case. It contained a shooting license and a few loose memoranda, but no money. Thurtell next produced Weare's silk purse.

In it were three sovereigns and some silver. They burned the purse upon the hearth together with the papers, and Thurtell divided the money.

"That's your share of the blunt," he said as he gave his mates six pounds apiece. He kept eleven pounds for himself, justifying the larger sum as compensation for the expense to which he had gone in renting the gig and purchasing the pistols.

"This is a bad look out," Probert said as he took his share. "This is hardly worth coming down for, Jack."

"It cannot be helped," Thurtell said. "I thought, Bill, we should have had a hundred or two at the least, but we must now make the best of it we can. This watch you must recollect, Bill, will fetch twenty or thirty pounds."

"Very true," Probert said, "and the gun, if it is good for any thing, will fetch ten pounds. Go, Hunt, and fetch the gun, and all the other things, and let's see what they are worth."

Hunt went to the stable and brought back the gun, a small box, and a carpetbag.

Probert took up the gun. "This is one of Manton's make," he said. "It will bring at least ten pounds." He then laid hold of the box. "This is the backgammon board you were speaking of, Jack."

"Yes," Thurtell said. "That is the board to pick up a flat with."

"Come, Jack, let's open the bag, there may be some money in that."

Thurtell took a knife and cut open the bag. In it were the clothes and traveling things Weare had brought down with him, together with his shooting gear, his loaded dice, and his false cards.*

--- • ---

---

* Hunt suspected that Thurtell and Probert misled him concerning the amount of money found on Weare's body in order that they might divide a larger sum between themselves. It is very likely that they did "well it" at Hunt's expense; but no proof of the deception has survived.

Perhaps no writer of his generation was more sensitive of the hellish breaches in existence than De Quincey, or more skilled in making their horror palpable to the reader. His account of his separation from the waif Ann, lost in the "mighty labyrinths of London," or of the woman who upon reaching a remote city encountered the evil footman, of a pale and bloodless complexion, whom she had dreamt she would find there, are overlaid with a horror more affecting than anything in the overt terror-poetry of the age. His lamentation for his friend Charles Lloyd, the mad poet, is one of the minor masterpieces so often met with in his writings. Lloyd "told me that his situation internally was always this—it seemed to him as if on some distant road he heard a dull trampling sound, and that he knew it, by a misgiving, to be the sound of some man, or party of men, continually advancing slowly, continually threatening, or continually accusing him." Once, when the fit was on him, he burst suddenly into tears on hearing the innocent voices of his own children laughing, and of one especially who was a favorite; and he "told me that sometimes, when this little child took his hand and led him passively about the garden, he had a feeling that prompted him (however weak and foolish it seemed) to call upon this child for protection; and that it seemed to him as if he might still escape, could he but sur-round himself only with children."

De Quincey was a pensioner of Morpheus, but although the dark light of opium is on his highest inspirations, it was not the only source of his genius. As much as the other Romantic prophets, he believed that sympathetic insight is a more efficient instrument in the search for truth than reason and analytical intelligence; and he advised his reader "never to pay any attention to his under-standing, when it stands in opposition to any other faculty of his mind." In his most perceptive moments, he was, it has been said, a psychological Champollion, whose feeling for the cross-weaving of beauty and horror in life enabled him to read more deeply (or, as he would have said, more "hieroglyphically") than others in the

Rosetta-Stone mystery of our being, written first to last, he said, in "the great alphabet of Nature."

The same sensitivity enabled De Quincey to fathom more deeply than any of his contemporaries the soul of the murderer, that type and figure of the diabolic in ordinary life. If we are to understand the murderer, he said, our "sympathy must be with *him*," by which "of course I mean a sympathy of comprehension, a sympathy by which we enter into his feelings, and are made to understand him,—not a sympathy of pity or approbation." This faculty of sympathetic perception would eventually bear fruit in the most penetrating of his murder essays, in which he showed how certain killers, craving an intoxication they could experience in no other way, murdered over and over again precisely in order to intensify an existence which would otherwise have seemed to them insipid.

———•———

Mrs. Probert, unable to sleep, went to the top of the stairs and, leaning over the railing, heard a sound like that of papers being rustled on a table and burnt in a fire. The conversation was all in whispers. It seemed to her that the men were trying on clothes. "I think that would fit you very well," she heard someone say in a low voice. Another said "We'll tell the boy there was a hare thrown on the cushion."

———•———

After they divided the spoils, Thurtell said that they must go and fetch the body and put it in the pond near the cottage.

Probert objected. "You shall not put it in the pond," he said. "It may ruin us."

Thurtell said it would lie there only for a short time, until he could arrange to dispose of it more effectually. But he found the corpse ponderous and returned to the cottage. "He is too heavy," he said. "Will you go along with me, Probert? I'll put the bridle on my horse and fetch him."

———•———

Mrs. Probert heard a door open and went to the window. It was, she remembered, a "very fine moonlight night." Two shadowy forms were going toward the stable. A moment later, one of them led out a horse.

———•———

They brought the body back by way of the garden gate. Thurtell led the horse; Probert held the sack to keep it from falling off. Every murder re-enacts the eternal mystery of evil; and like the first transgression in paradise, the re-enactment gains in power if there is a woman in it, a garden, and a snake or two. Mrs. Probert "heard something dragged, as it seemed, very heavily." She went to the window and saw them taking the sack through the garden to the pond. She lost sight of them; but after an interval she heard "a hollow noise, like a heap of stones being thrown into a pit."

CHAPTER TWELVE

A Deeper Abyss

Better be with the dead,
Whom we, to gain our peace, have sent to peace,
Than in the torture of the mind to lie
In restless ecstasy. . . .

—*Shakespeare*

A little after six o'clock the next morning, John Harrington, a laboring man, and his partner were at work in Gill's Hill Lane, engaged in widening the road. Two men passed by them, a tall one and a short one. They went down the lane and stopped not far from a maple tree. Harrington watched as they "grabbled in the hedge."

When they came back up the lane, the tall man spoke to Harrington's partner. "Are you going to widen this lane?" he asked.

"Yes, as wide as we can."

"I was nearly capsized here last night."

"I hope you were not hurt."

"Oh, no, we were not thrown out."

The two men went on their way, and Harrington and his partner resumed their work. When, afterwards, Harrington went over to the place where the men had grabbled, he found a hole in the hedge and a quantity of blood. Something in the cart-rut caught his eye. It was a knife. It had two blades, one of which was broken, and it was covered with blood.

When Mr. Nicholls of Battlers Green came up the lane, Harrington showed him the knife. They searched among the brambles, and Harrington found a pistol. There was clotted gore on it, in which some hairs had become stuck.

———•———

Susan the cook was on her way to the kitchen to get breakfast ready when she met Thurtell and Hunt coming up the steps from the garden. Their boots were dirty.

———•———

After breakfast, the roan gray was harnessed to the gig, and Probert brought out Weare's carpetbag, backgammon box, and gun. Thurtell said he would come down the next day to dispose of the body for good. He and Hunt drove off, and Probert went for a walk with his dog, intent on retrieving the knife and pistol. But the presence of Harrington and his partner, who were still at work on the road, disconcerted him. He wished them good morning and said it was a good job they were doing, before he turned around and went back to the cottage.

———•———

Thurtell got out of the gig in Oxford Street, fearful lest he should meet Upson, the Bow Street officer who had a warrant against him for defrauding the County Fire Office. He made his way by back streets to the Coach and Horses. Hunt drove on to his lodgings in King Street, Golden Square, where he hid Thurtell's greatcoat under the bed, for although it had been copiously sponged, it was still "a great deal stained with blood." He then returned the horse and gig and walked to Conduit Street, where he met Thurtell. Together they went to an ironmonger's in Warwick Street to purchase a spade. Afterwards, they dined in the Coach and Horses; Hunt, in high spirits, told the company that he and Jack had been netting game, and had left Probert holding the bag. "We Turpin lads," he said, "can do the trick."*

———•———

On Sunday morning, Thurtell and Hunt drove back to Probert's cottage. Hunt took out the spade and threw it over the hedge to conceal it. When Probert came out, Hunt asked him whether there was a room in which he could change his clothes. Probert showed him to a room upstairs, and a little later Hunt came down dressed in a black coat and waistcoat. Thurtell smiled and told Hunt that he looked very smart, quite like a Turpin. He then jested that Probert "would never do for a Turpin."

Probert and Thurtell went down to the garden and the pond. Thurtell asked whether the body had risen. Probert said no—it would lie there for a month. When they returned to the house, they found a neighbor, Mr. Heward, at the door. He was on his way to Mr. Nicholls's farm at Battlers Green; there was a rumor afoot that something had happened in Gill's Hill Lane the other night. Probert went down with him to Battlers Green.

---

* Dick Turpin, poacher, thief, highwayman, and murderer, was hanged on the gallows at Knavesmire, York, in April 1739.

CHAPTER THIRTEEN

Turpin Lads

It had been good for that man if he had not been born.

Matthew 26:24

They were now doomed; the deed could not be undone. When Probert returned from Battlers Green, he took Hunt into the garden and told him of Mr. Nicholls's saying to him that a gun had been fired in Gill's Hill Lane on Friday night. Another farmer said he had heard pistol shots, while still another heard groans and a man crying out "O John, for God's sake, spare me. . . ." Such was his fright, Probert said, that his hand began to tremble, and he was afraid he would drop the glass of gin-and-water Mr. Nicholls had given him; but he concealed his agitation and asked Mr. Nicholls what time the shots had been heard.

"About eight o'clock."

"I suppose some of your friends wanted to frighten you, sir."

When Thurtell came into the garden, Probert repeated the story.

"Then I'm baked," Thurtell said.

"I'm afraid it's a bad job," Probert continued, "for Nicholls seems to know all about it. I am very sorry it ever happened here. I'm afraid it will be my ruin."

"Never mind," Thurtell said, "they can do nothing with you."

"The body must be immediately taken up from my pond, John."

"I'll tell you what I'll do—when they are all gone to bed, you and I'll take and bury him."

Probert shook his head, saying it would be "bad if they buried him in the garden."

"I'll bury him where you nor no one else can find him."

"Probert," Hunt said, "they can do nothing with you, or me either, because neither of us was at the murder."

———•———

They dined in Probert's cottage and afterwards played whist; but the game ended when Thurtell threw up his cards, saying they ran cross. He sat up late with Hunt, and when the house was quiet they went out to dig the grave. They began to shovel the dirt with the spade, but the work was hard, and the barking of the dogs unnerved them. It seemed to them that someone was lurking nearby, observing.

The next morning—it was Monday, October 27—Jack showed Probert the grave he had begun to dig. He confessed that he had second thoughts about the wisdom of burying the body, and was inclined instead to take it away and dispose of it elsewhere. He might, for instance, take it to Manchester Buildings, and when the opportunity arose throw it into the Thames. If the corpse should float on the river, it would, he reasoned, be so changed as to be unrecognizable.

Probert expressed a fear that the boy Addis had seen too much. Thurtell said he would take him to London on the pretext of finding him a "place"—a job—there. He and Joe would then come back to Radlett and take the body away. "That," he said, "will be the better for you altogether."

The boy Addis was duly taken to London, and in the evening Thurtell and Hunt, who had shaved off his whiskers, returned to the cottage for the last time. Probert was in a frenzy. There were ominous reports in the neighborhood, and he wanted to abandon the cottage altogether.

When supper was finished, Thurtell and Probert went out, leaving Hunt to entertain Mrs. Probert. They drew the sack from the pond and took out the body. After they cut away the clothes, they left the body naked on the greensward and went to fetch Hunt. When they had put the body back into the sack, they dragged it to the garden gate and put it into the gig. Thurtell and Hunt climbed in and drove off; Probert burned the clothes and scattered the remnants about the hedges.

———•———

On the same night that Thurtell and Hunt threw Weare's body into the brook at Elstree, Sir Walter Scott was at Abbotsford, his estate near Melrose in the Scottish Borders, looking forward to the feast he and Lady Scott were to give their tenants and retainers on the morrow, in thanksgiving for the harvest.

Sir Walter was fifty-two in October 1823. In two decades of literary toil, he had changed the face of Gothic romance. Horace Walpole and Mrs. Radcliffe had set their romances in imaginary Italies; Scott wrote about places he knew intimately. As a young lawyer he had ridden out to the wilder districts of the Scottish Borders, hoping "to pick up some of the ancient riding ballads" which were said to be still preserved in those remote regions. Saul, seeking asses, found a kingdom; Scott, hunting up old songs in shepherds' huts, found the materials for a literary empire. In his "raids," as he called them, into the unfrequented recesses of the Borders, he gathered up a rich plunder of minstrelsy and balladry, myth and folklore, the forgotten music of a people. In 1802, at thirty-one, he brought out his *Minstrelsy of the Scottish Border*, which contained the first fruits of his excursions into Auld Scotland. Three years later, in 1805, he published a verse romance, *The Lay of the Last Minstrel*, based loosely on Border legends of a pernicious goblin; in 1814 came the first of his prose-romances, *Waverley*.

The interest of a romance, Scott said, "turns upon marvelous or uncommon incidents." The trick lay in making what is marvelous and uncommon credible to the reader. Scott's closeness to the sources of his material gave his tales of the marvelous a plausibility unrivaled by the other romancers of the age and made him famous. For it was an age hungry for credible romance. Life was everywhere becoming less musical and more mechanical, and Scott's fantasies filled the vacuum of *ennui* that opened up, in respectable English households, between dinner and tea-time.

He supplied, too, just the right touch of erotic horror in his books. His picture of Lucy Ashton, in *The Bride of Lammermoor*, crouching, on her wedding night, in torn and bloody night-clothes, anticipates the gore and lewdness of the Hollywood horror movie; but in deference to the taste of the age, Scott was less explicit, in carnal and country matters, than the artists of our own unlaced days are apt to be. *The Bride of Lammermoor* is probably Scott's most effective Gothic romance; but like all his work, it is prosey and artificially heightened. His image of Lucy as an "exulting demoniac," gibbering in a "wild paroxysm of insanity," paints not half so lurid a picture in the mind as the loin of pork in Probert's cottage.

Scott himself was never satisfied with his romances, and he sought a more substantial simulacrum of the Gothic in Abbotsford itself. To a friend, he called the house "a sort of romance in architecture" and quoted a line from Coleridge's *Christabel*:

A sight to dream of, not to tell!

"I never saw anything handsomer," he said, "than the grouping of towers, chimneys, etc. upon the roof, when seen at a proper distance." And yet it did not signify; the skulls, the suits of armor, the oaken chairs, were they not, finally, so much Gothic gimcrackery? Still Scott did not give up: the master romancer persisted in his search for an authentic Gothicism. And curiously enough, he was soon to find it—in the low-witted deviltry of Jack Thurtell.

———•———

On Tuesday, Mr. Nicholls of Battlers Green went to Watford to see the magistrates. He brought with him the knife and pistol John Harrington had found in Gill's Hill Lane, and showed the officer what he had discovered when he put a long nail into the barrel of the pistol—something like brains. A short time later, the authorities took Probert into custody. He gave them the names of his weekend house guests, and on Wednesday morning, George Ruthven, one of the last of the Bow Street Runners, went over to Conduit Street.

"Is that you, Jack?" he asked as he came into Thurtell's room in the Coach and Horses. "John, my boy, I want you."

"What for, George?"

"Never mind; I'll tell you presently."

Thurtell was taken into custody without incident. Later in the day, Ruthven apprehended Joe Hunt in his lodgings in King Street, Golden Square.

———•———

After undergoing examination in Bow Street, Thurtell and Hunt were conveyed to Watford. Hunt, in an effort to save himself, told the magistrates that he knew where the body of the murdered man lay, and led them to the brook near Hill Slough.

CHAPTER FOURTEEN

The Last Days of Thurtell

The guerdon of their murder they had got.

—*Keats*

I n December, the General Session of Our Lord the King of Oyer and Terminer in and for the County of Hertford—better known as the Hertford Assizes—was convened in the town of Hertford. The judges were conducted by the High Sheriff to the courthouse, and the court was opened. Afterwards, the judges repaired to church to hear divine service. At noon the court met again, with Mr. Justice Park* presiding, and the grand jurors were sworn. The foreman was the Right Honorable William Lamb, Member of Parliament for Peterborough, who had ridden over that

---

* Sir James Alan Park. Born at Edinburgh in 1763; educated at Northampton Grammar School and Lincoln's Inn; elevated to the bench as a judge of Common Pleas in 1816 and knighted in the same year; died in 1838.

morning from his country seat, Brocket Hall (now a golf club). He was the husband of Lady Caroline, the pretty exhibitionist whom Byron had briefly loved or coveted: a decade hence, he would be Prime Minister. Like Mr. Lamb, the other jurors were, in the words of Mr. Justice Park, "gentlemen of the first dignity, rank, and respectability" in the county. Satisfied of the truth of the indictments preferred against the accused, the jurors found "a true bill," and the three men were committed for trial.

—•—

The trial took place in January. Probert, who had turned Crown's evidence in exchange for a promise to be let off, testified against Thurtell and Hunt. Only once was the solemnity of the proceeding momentarily softened into humor. Susan the cook testified that, on the night the murder was committed, she had been ordered to prepare supper. Mr. Broderick, junior counsel for the Crown, asked her whether the supper was "postponed."

"I don't know," she replied, "it was pork."

Thurtell's bearing and conduct, in his last extremity, won all hearts, even those of his jailers, and when he was called to speak in his own defense, his words—prepared, for the most part, by others, but committed by him to memory—very nearly persuaded the jury to acquit him. Dressed, a writer for *The London Magazine* observed, in a "plum-colored frock-coat, with a drab waistcoat and gilt buttons," he cut an impressive figure "in frame, face, eye, and daring," and in his peroration he "clung to every separate word with an earnestness which we cannot describe, as though every syllable had the power to buoy up his sinking life." "Cut me not off," he beseeched the jurors, "in the very summer of my life. . . . I stand before you as before my God, overwhelmed with misfortunes, but unconscious of crime; and while you decide on my future destiny, I earnestly entreat you to remember my last solemn declaration; I am innocent, so help me God!"

The poet Keats's friend, John Hamilton Reynolds, who was present in the courtroom, came away with the image of a "strong desperate man playing the hero of the tragic trial, as at a play." But the actor's performance, though stirring, was not convincing; and the jury, after deliberating for half an hour, found Thurtell guilty of having "feloniously, and with malice aforethought," murdered Weare.

It "cannot but give great compunction to every feeling mind," Mr. Justice Park said from the bench, "that a person who, from his conduct this day, has shewn that he was born with capacity for better things" should nevertheless have been "guilty of so foul and detestable a crime." He then put the black cap upon his head and addressed the prisoner at the bar. "The sentence of law which I have to pronounce upon you, John Thurtell, according to the statute, is this—that you, John Thurtell, be taken to the place from whence you came, and from thence that you be taken on Friday, the ninth instant, to a place of execution, and that you be hanged by the neck till you be dead. . . ."

———•———

Far away, in Scotland, Sir Walter Scott was absorbed in the case of Thurtell. In "all Sir Walter's many readings in murder literature," Carlyle's friend David Mather Masson wrote, he seems never "to have come upon any murder that more fascinated him." He assiduously collected newspaper articles, pamphlets, and chapbooks relating to the crime, and had them bound together in a variorum volume. In moments of funk, he turned to the collection for relief; and after the collapse of his fortunes, when two publishing firms in which he was a silent partner failed for more than a quarter of a million pounds, the variorum became not only a diversion but a consolation. "Very unsatisfactory to-day," he wrote in his journal in July 1826. "Sleepy, stupid, indolent—finished arranging the books, and after that was totally useless, unless it can be called study that I slumbered for three or four hours over a variorum edition of the Gill's-Hill tragedy.* Admirable recipe for low spirits."

His fascination with a crime that revealed so much of the skull beneath the skin of human life did not abate, and in May 1828 he visited the scene of the crime. He marveled at the "strange intricate combination of narrow roads" he found in Hertfordshire, "winding and turning among oaks and other large timber, just like pathways cut through a forest. They wind and turn in so singular a manner, and resemble each other so much, that a stranger would have difficulty to make way amongst them."

Scott rode through the labyrinth of lanes to the cottage itself. "The dirt of the present habitation equaled its wretched desolation," he wrote, "and a truculent-looking hag, who showed us the place, and received a half-crown, looked not unlike the natural intimate of such a mansion. She indicated as much herself, saying the landlord dismantled the place because no respectable person would live there."

The garden was overgrown, the pond a mere green swamp. Scott remembered Wordsworth's lines:

> A merry spot, 'tis said, in days of yore,
> But something ails it now—the place is curs'd.

"Indeed the whole history of the murder, and the scenes which ensued," Scott concluded, "are strange pictures of desperate and short-sighted wickedness. The feasting—the singing—the murderer with his hands still bloody round the neck of one of the females—the watch-chain of the murdered man, argue the utmost apathy."

In his collection of the printed reports of the trial, Scott "took care always," his son-in-law, John Gibson Lockhart, wrote, "to have the contemporary ballads and prints bound up with them. He admired particularly this verse of Mr. Hook's broadside—

---

* The murder of Weare was variously referred to as the "Radlett Murder," the "Elstree Murder," and the "Gill's Hill Tragedy."

They cut his throat from ear to ear,
His brains they battered in;
His name was Mr. William Weare.
He dwelt in Lyon's Inn.

———•———

Thurtell was hanged on January 9, 1824, on the gallows in front of Hertford Gaol, conducting himself to the end with manly firmness. It is said that his last words, spoken after he learned that the boxer Spring had won the fight against Langham, were "I am glad of it, for Spring is a good fellow."

Hunt, who had been found guilty of aiding and abetting his friend in the murder of Weare, was also sentenced to die upon the scaffold. But at the last moment, he was spared: his sentence was commuted on the advice of Mr. Peel, the Home Secretary, and he was transported to Botany Bay. In Australia he became a changed man and was made custodian of the assize court at Bathurst, New South Wales. He died in 1861, if not in the odor of sanctity, at least with the respect of his neighbors.

Probert's destiny was less happy. He was shunned as a treacherous wretch who had escaped a just retribution by peaching on his mates, and he was unable to obtain employment. In 1825 he was accused of stealing a horse. He was tried at the Old Bailey, found guilty, and sentenced to death. Addressing the court, he said that "since the calamitous event that took place at Hertford, I have been a lost man, and at times on the eve of self-destruction." He was hanged on the gallows at Newgate in April 1825.

It was the fate of Mrs. Probert to live out the remainder of her life as a "hempen widow," whose husband had been hanged. She took to calling herself Mrs. Heath, and moved to Cheltenham. She was found drowned in the Chelt in the autumn of 1857, not far from Barrett's Mill.

PART TWO

The Mystery of the Mutilated Corpse

Torn limb from limb, he spreads his horrid feast. . . .

—*Pope*

CHAPTER ONE

The Parcel in the Canterbury Villas

While smooth Adonis from his native rock
Ran purple to the sea, supposed with blood
Of Thammuz yearly wounded . . .

—Milton

Toward the end of December 1836, a bricklayer was engaged in building a garden wall for the Canterbury Villas, a cluster of newly erected houses in the Edgware Road. About two o'clock, he observed something dark lying behind an as-yet-unlaid paving stone. On going over to it, he saw what appeared to be a sack of coarse canvas. He removed the stone and found the sack stiffly fixed in a pool of reddish ooze.

The supervisor was summoned and the parcel removed from the gore. Wrapped in rags (a piece of twilled jean patched with nankeen, a scrap of huckaback toweling, and a cotton shawl) was the remnant of a human body. The head and legs were missing and appeared to have been sawn off; the arms and hands, however, remained. Together with the flesh and the bones, there was also, in the sack, a quantity of blood-stained mahogany shavings.

The constable was called, and at his direction the remains were taken to the police station. The parish surgeon, Dr. Gilbert Finlay Girdwood, pronounced them to be those of a woman in the middle of life, and he conjectured that, up to the time of her death, she had been in good health. From the condition of her arms and hands, he supposed that she had for many years worked hard at some form of manual labor.

The carving of a human being joint from joint has long occupied a special place in the cabinet of horror. The myths of Greece, Egypt, and Mesopotamia abound in extravagant mutilations, the flesh-carvings undergone by such colorful sufferers as Orpheus, Osiris, and Thammuz. The Christian martyrologies are not less copious of sliced and shredded flesh, and may even have excited a deeper revulsion, at least among those who believed that the butchery of one's body was an obstacle to the salvation of one's soul. For if one's vile body was to be made "like to His glorious body" (so the popular superstition ran), it had to be buried whole, preferably with the feet pointing toward Jerusalem.

It is true that, in the year of grace 1836, the fear inspired by Judgment Day was grown much fainter among the English than it had been of old. In the dawn of the steamship, the railway, and the first Reform Bill, England seemed to bask in the very sunshine of Reason and Progress. Yet some vestige of the old religious terror remained and perhaps accounts for the hysteria that colored London's reaction to the gruesome discovery in the Edgware Road.* Clearly, new forms of fiendishness were incubating in Albion, in spite of the enlightened exertions of Lord Grey and Sir Robert Peel; there were even prophets abroad in the land, like Carlyle and De Quincey, who went so far as to suggest that Reason and Progress themselves were not all they were cracked up to be.

---

* Six years earlier, the murder and dismemberment of Celia Holloway at Brighton had produced a similar sensation. James Catnach, the gutter poet and catchpenny printer, published a ballad, *The Lamentation and Confession of John William Holloway*, which purported to be the husband's account of the killing:

> In Donkey Row I took a house, and there enticed my wife,
> 'Twas then by strangulation that I took away her life:
> Alas, a tender womb-snug babe I murdered in the strife,
> And cut the flesh to pieces with a freshly sharpened knife.
>
> I chopped her up and—Oh!—it was a most appalling sight:
> I wheeled her all the way to Preston under cover of the night.
> Her head and arms, her legs and thighs, were rudely sawèd off,
> And with the trunk two thighs I buried in the turf of Lover's Walk.

When, in the spring of 2009, pieces of the body of Jeffrey Howe, the victim in the "jigsaw" murder, were found north of London, the police kept the "harrowing details" of the dismemberment from the public "so as not to spread panic."

CHAPTER TWO

Gory Locks

O heaven! that one might read the book of fate,
And see how chances mock,
And changes fill the cup of alteration
With divers liquors! O, if this were seen,
The happiest youth—viewing his progress through,
What perils past, what crosses to ensue—
Wouldst shut the book, and sit him down and die.

—*Shakespeare*

Ten days after the discovery of the remains in the Edgware Road, a barge in the Regent's Canal was navigating the lock near Ben Johnson's Fields, close by Stepney Green in east London. The floodgate would not close. "It's a dead dog," the lock-keeper said, "ease the gate." He (or his assistant) thrust the hitcher, or grappling hook, into the water; but the impediment, when it was drawn out, proved to be not the carcass of a dog, but the head of a woman; her gory locks were remarkably long.

The grisly object was brought to the bone-house of Stepney Churchyard, where a local surgeon, Dr. John Birtwhistle of Mile End Road, examined it. The jaw had been fractured during the lock-keeper's attempts to close the floodgate, and one of the cheeks had been pierced by the grappling hook. But it seemed to Dr. Birtwhistle probable that the contusion about the right eye had been made while the woman was yet alive.

"It was what I should call a tremendous black eye," Dr. Birtwhistle said, and "was caused in my opinion before death." The cervical vertebrae immediately below the skull, he observed, had been sawn clean through; and when, afterwards, he compared the saw marks to those of the remains from the Edgware Road, he found that they fitted together as neatly as the pieces of a jigsaw puzzle.

London was more alarmed than ever. Before the discovery of the severed head, it had been just possible to dismiss the mutilated flesh in the Edgware Road as merely the fragment of a cadaver carelessly disposed of by medical men, who in the 1830s were dissecting carcasses at a rapid clip. The Anatomy Act of 1832 had rescinded ancient taboos, and with its passage the anatomists had ceased to be dependent, in their search for susceptible corpses, on the remains of executed murderers, as they had been under older statutes.* They were now free to exercise their art upon a more plentiful class of bodies, those of the innocent but unclaimed dead—paupers, for the most part, whose loved ones could not afford the expense of burial, or who had died unloved. But with the fishing up of the head in the

---

* Before the passage of this legislation, a number of anatomists had conspired with grave robbers and even murderers in the quest for cadavers, practices which came to light after the murders committed by Messrs. Burke and Hare in 1828. An Edinburgh physician, Dr. Knox, was implicated in the traffic in corpses but was not prosecuted; his infamy, however, lived on in the couplet: "Burke's the butcher, Hare's the thief, / Knox the boy who buys the beef."

Regent's Canal, it was only too evident that the poor dead woman had not been the object of a legitimate anatomical curiosity. She had met with foul play, and at the hands of someone who had attempted to conceal his crime by the partition of her corpse and the artful distribution of its parts.

On February 2, a third discovery was made. A laborer near Coldharbour Lane, Camberwell, was cutting osiers (a kind of willow used in making baskets) when he saw a bundle lying partly submerged in a ditch. A toe protruded from it. When afterwards the bundle was opened, it was found to contain a pair of human legs. Dr. Girdwood, who examined them, was of the opinion that they had once formed a piece with the trunk from the Edgware Road and the head fished out of the Regent's Canal.

With each revelation the mystery deepened, and the consternation of the public grew. The Metropolitan Police, which as a result of Sir Robert Peel's legislation had superseded "Mr. Fielding's People," the Bow Street Runners, diligently investigated. The new police officers, known as "Peelers" or "Bobbies," went out into the murk of the London winter wrapped in oilskin capes and, threading their way through the slums and rookeries, sought clues to the identity of the killer. But their inquiries were in vain.

CHAPTER THREE

William and Maria Gay

Our sorrow is the inverted image of our nobleness.
—*Thomas Carlyle*

There was in London at this time a Norfolk man named William Gay. At the beginning of 1837, Mr. Gay was perhaps forty years of age; he did not know the precise day or even year of his birth. He was employed as an assistant to a a pawnbroker in Goodge Street called Mrs. Blanchard; he and his wife, Maria, had a room above the shop.

The couple had come to London two years before. Like many others freshly arrived in the metropolis, they were doing their best to adapt themselves to a new age. They had grown up in the English countryside, amid thatched cottages and village greens; but the England of their childhood was passing away; Oliver Goldsmith had pronounced its epitaph so early as 1770, in his poem *The Deserted Village.*

In London, the Gays encountered the new England that was rapidly superseding the old one into which they had been born. It is an England that is even now familiar to us, preserved as it is in the engravings of Gustave Doré and in the early daguerreotypes, with their weird tints and unearthly chiaroscuros. It is the England of the young Dickens, whose *Oliver Twist* was just then appearing in *Bentley's* magazine—an England that had for its chiefest symbol London itself, choking under its pall of smoke and soot and river mist. London in those days had a Gothic morbidity peculiar to itself; Doré was to bring it out in his engravings, and Dickens in his books—the sense that there lurked, in the murk and shadow just beyond the reach of the tallow-light, an unspeakable beastliness.*

The days were short now, and darkened by yellow fogs. At midday there was "hardly light enough," Thomas Carlyle said, to see one's way in Chelsea. Farther east, in the heart of the metropolis, it was darker still: "beyond Hyde Park Corner, think what it must be,—Erebus, Nox and the great deep of gases, miasmata, soot and despair. . . ."

William and Maria Gay brightened the gloom with newspaper accounts of the latest demonism to afflict the capital. The mystery of the mutilated corpse was for them, as it was for so much of Londonry, a diverting story, one with a quantity of hellishness sufficient to beguile a long winter evening. The truth is, William and Maria Gay needed diversion. Newly arrived in London as they were, they had not many friends—had perhaps not had time to make them, for in those days working people were commonly about their business twelve hours a day, six days a week. When once Mr.

---

* In 1837, a creature of diabolic countenance known as Spring-Heeled Jack was said to be preying upon lone servant girls in London, swooping down upon them in forlorn places and ripping their gowns with his claws. Such stories were widely credited in an age in which ghosts and ogres and scaly things in their naïvest forms still haunted men's imaginations. Matthew Arnold told the story of a man who ventured to ask the poet William Blake whether he had ever seen a ghost, and "was surprised when the famous seer, who ought, one might think, to have seen so many, answered frankly, 'Only once!'"

Gay was asked about those with whom he habitually conversed, he replied, "I hold very little conversation with any one."

Boredom and curiosity might have induced William and Maria Gay to take an interest in the anonymous corpse of a murdered woman; but by degrees the sensations of pity and pleasure which appalling acts naturally arouse in the human heart gave way to the apprehension that they themselves might be closely related to the victim.

CHAPTER FOUR

Hannah Brown

Yes, yes; a very good woman, in the main.

—*Lillo*

"I should think my sister was forty-seven years of age, or about that," William Gay said. "She was much older than me—I am only guessing at her age—I do not know my own age." Hannah left home when William was a boy, to go into the service of one of the Norfolk magnates, Lord Wodehouse of Crimley Hall. Later she went up to London and was cook in the house of Mr. Barclay, of the banking family. In due course, she found herself caught in the "parson's mousetrap," having wedded a shoemaker named Brown, with whom she went to live in the country. An unsatisfactory man, this Brown, living an unsatisfactory but, as it fell out, sharply abbreviated life. He took ship for Jamaica, intent on claiming a property that had been bequeathed to him, and was washed overboard.

Hannah Brown, a widow now, returned to London and her former occupations. She kept house, at different times, for an anchor-smith in the Docklands, a hatter in the Strand, sundry others. But she chafed at the constraints of a mop-squeezing life. She had always been a frugal woman, and through her thrift had accumulated a small capital. This she used to purchase a mangle, a device for wringing the water out of laundered clothes. Henceforth she would get her living by taking in other people's washing. She "earned her bread by very hard labour," her sister-in-law Maria Gay said, for "a mangle requires power." But the mangle also conferred power, and Hannah Brown hereafter lived, not as a dependent servant, but as an independent woman.

Still she remains dim to us; comes, at best, into an imperfect focus. She had a gray eye, a "delicate" skin, and (what was unusual in those days) a "very nice set of teeth." Her hair, which she wore long, was still brown, though "mingled with a little grey." A "tall and rather good-looking woman," all in all, with a fund of self-respecting dignities and femininities. She possessed a dress of black silk with a black veil, and a white dress of jaconet muslin with a white veil. A silk cloak, a feathered boa, and a pair of Cornelian ear-drops are also distinctly mentioned.

Nor was a more valuable species of commodity wanting to her: Hannah Brown had friends. Mrs. Blanchard, her brother's employer, had been her chum from childhood, as had Sarah Ullathorne, the wife of a prosperous baker in the Strand. Her acquaintance with Evan and Hannah Davis, a couple who lived in Bartholomew Close above St. Paul's, had ripened into a deeper intimacy. They were probably her closest friends, and she had sometimes joined them, in her white dress, on summer excursions to Gravesend, in those days a popular bathing place. Yet, for all that, there was a vacancy in her life that friendship could not fill; for this "tall, fine, genteel, respectable-looking female" (so Mrs. Davis's daughter thought her) was a woman, in the language of the Prayer Book, with a "womb that never bare" and "paps which never gave suck." A "remarkable peculiarity in her formation of body," it was said, made it "impossible that she could ever have been a mother."

It seems likely that Hannah Brown drew on her friendship with Mrs. Blanchard to obtain a place for her brother William in the shop in Goodge Street. At all events, she lived with William and Maria in their apartment in Mrs. Blanchard's house at the beginning of 1835, staying for two or three weeks, possibly as long as a month. But there had been a quarrel. "We had words," Maria Gay recalled. "My husband was at variance with his sister . . . they had rather differed. . . . The variance took place while she lived with us—that was the reason we parted. . . ."

Hannah found lodgings of her own, in the kitchen belowstairs in a house in nearby Union Street. But the breach in the blood-relation was never mended, and whenever Hannah encountered her brother's wife in the street, she cut her dead.

CHAPTER FIVE

Mr. Gay's Inquiries

Art thou not the man that I found crying, without
the walls of the City of Destruction?
              —Bunyan, *The Pilgrim's Progress*

There were more than a million souls in greater London;
the odds were distinctly against it. And yet, there was
something odd about it. When had they last seen their
sister Hannah? Before Christmas, surely. Yes, the Thursday
before—Thursday, the twenty-second. It was William who saw her;
he was in the shop in Goodge Street when Hannah came in. As was
their custom now, the siblings exchanged not a word with one other;
Hannah made it clear that she had come to see not her brother but
his employer, her friend Mrs. Blanchard. Hannah's mood, however,
was far from sour; in fact she was distinctly cheerful—in fact, she
was to be married!

Within the week, William had further news of his sister. On the Tuesday after Christmas, a man whom he had never seen before came into the shop. It was "about seven o'clock or so—it was candle-light," William remembered. "I was not exactly in the shop—I came from the low kitchen."

Mrs. Blanchard was behind the counter when the man came in. "I heard him speaking to her," William recalled, "and telling her the wedding was put off, that he had investigated into the character of Mrs. Brown." When he agreed to marry her, he said, he "thought that she had" property, for such was "the report he had heard from some people." In fact she "had no property," and had "run him in debt at the tally-shop" in Long Acre. He had "had a few words" with Mrs. Brown over this, and afterwards they had thought it best not to marry.

Mrs. Blanchard gestured toward William. "This is Mrs. Brown's brother," she said; "won't you walk in?"

"No," the man replied. "I am in a hurry."

The "countenance of the man changed," William recalled, and he walked off into the December night "saying something which I could not understand."

———•———

The London night in Goodge Street is familiar to readers of English literature. It is the De Quinceyian night of a metropolis coated with a "paste composed of ancient soot and superannuated rain," a Dickensian night of candles flaring in the windows, of fog pouring in at every chink and keyhole, of houses that seem mere phantoms in the mist.

Earlier Londons are not so accessible. One can picture—just— Boswell and Dr. Johnson, in the eighteenth century, dining at the Mitre, or Addison drinking coffee at Button's. But the vision is dim; one does not know those Londons as one does the London of Dickens and De Quincey. *They* make the reader feel of London what Balzac makes him feel of Paris: that it is not merely a city, but a living organism, one that possesses not only a personality but a soul of its own. Paris, Balzac says in *Le Père Goriot*, is "an ocean that no line can plumb. You may survey its surface and describe it; but no matter how numerous and painstaking the toilers in this sea, there will always be lonely and unexplored regions in its depths, caverns unknown, flowers and pearls, monsters of the deep overlooked or forgotten by the divers of literature." It is the same with the London of Dickens and De Quincey. Like Balzac, they are late-Romantic personalities, and like him they have the late-Romantic intuition of the presence, in apparently mundane things, of infinite mystery, of spiritual power, of invisible kingdoms of beauty and terror, of submerged realms of supernatural beastliness and grace.* The real city, for the Romantic writer, is shadowed by one that is unreal, visionary, a place where "ghosts in the open air hang upon the sleeves of the passer-by."

The ghost of Hannah Brown was the latest specter to figure in the metropolitan nightmare. There is a traditional belief that it was Maria Gay who, through some feminine prevoyance, first suspected that it was the severed corpse of her sister-in-law that had spooked the city. According to one report, she would not let her husband rest until he had made inquiries; at all events, it is certain that he did eventually make them. He went first to his sister's landlady, Mrs. Corney, in Union Street. She told him that Hannah had slept away on the Friday before Christmas, but had returned the next day—Christmas Eve—in a hackney coach. There had been a man with her, who had helped her retrieve her boxes and trunks. Afterwards

---

* The late-Romantic prose of Dickens and De Quincey illuminates the London of the 1830s and '40s in much the same way that the Oxford Movement illuminates the religion of the period and the Young England Movement the politics. Each was in part a reaction against what John Henry Newman, the foremost figure of the Oxford Movement, called the "dry and superficial character" of the thought of the eighteenth century: each sought to replace it with a "deeper philosophy" of the soul.

they had driven off. Mrs. Corney never saw Hannah again; the following Wednesday, another of her lodgers, Mrs. Hawksworth, brought her the key to Hannah's room, which she said had been given her by a strange boy. Later that day, Mrs. Corney and her husband inspected the apartment; they found nothing in it but an empty birdcage. It had belonged to the late Mr. Brown, before he had fallen into his watery grave.

———•———

Mr. Gay's inquiries next took him eastward, to Bartholomew Close, where he called upon Evan and Hannah Davis. Evan Davis was a cabinetmaker and upholsterer; he and his wife had gotten to know Hannah Brown through Evan's sister. (The two women had once been servants together in the same house.) The acquaintance had deepened into affection, and Hannah Brown had been in the habit of calling frequently on Hannah Davis.

Evan Davis remembered how, shortly before Christmas, he was in his workshop when his wife called him into the parlor. There he found Hannah and a man upon whom he had never before laid eyes; Hannah introduced him only as her "beau." He was stoutish of figure, well-dressed, voluble, with the air of one who thought himself a person of some consequence in the world. Evan welcomed him warmly and proposed that they go over to the Hand & Shears for a drink. Over a pint of ale, Hannah's beau spoke of America. He had a farm of a thousand acres there, at Hudson's Bay, and planned to return to it after Christmas.

Hannah and her man came again to Bartholomew Close on the Thursday before Christmas, the same day William Gay saw his sister for the last time in Goodge Street. After a drink in the parlor with the women, the men went over to the French Horn, a public house close by. Hannah's beau was again full of talk of America, the "grand place it was, and the railroads there, and his farm," which was "a beautiful place." The two couples supped together in Bartholomew Close and afterwards seated themselves in the parlor.

"Well," Hannah's beau said as he sat beside her on the sofa, "we may as well tell you our intentions, as we are not children . . . we intend to get married on Sunday morning (Christmas Day)." It was all arranged; the banns had been entered by the parish clerk, and been duly published by the minister; the wedding clothes had been procured. All that remained was to find a man to give the bride away and a maid to attend her to the altar. The ornamental offices were soon filled; Evan Davis would give the bride away, and the Davises' eldest daughter, who was also named Hannah, would be the bridesmaid. In a handsome gesture, Evan offered to give a dinner to the wedding party after the ceremony. Hannah expressed to Mrs. Davis her hope that she would come to see her in her new home in Carpenter's Place, Camberwell. Of course the "state of the house," she said, would not be "very nice," for they would be "going away soon to America," to the farm at Hudson's Bay.

The party broke up about ten o'clock; but not before it was agreed that they would all meet again on Christmas Day at the Angel in Camberwell, from whence they would make their way to St. Giles, where the marriage was to take place.

———•———

But the four of them never did meet again. Two days later, on Christmas Eve, a north wind was blowing when, about ten o'clock, Hannah's fiancé appeared on the Davises' doorstep in Bartholomew Close. Had they seen Hannah? No, Mrs. Davis said, not since the breaking up of the party Thursday night. Whereupon the man said he had "closely investigated" Hannah's affairs and discovered that she had deceived him "with regard to her property." The match had therefore been broken off, as it would not do "to plunge headlong into poverty."

He "went away much agitated," Mrs. Davis remembered, and his "countenance presented an aspect of such peculiarity" that she remarked upon it to her husband.*

———•———

Sunday, March 12, 1837, dawned clear and frosty. William Gay crossed the Thames and made his way southward to his sister's last known address, 6 Carpenter's Place, Windmill Lane, Camberwell. The woman who answered the door told him that the previous occupant had gone away in January. Where had he gone? Not very far, the woman supposed, for he owned the house and had recently told her that he would send someone round next week to collect the rent. Before taking the house, she and her family had lived at 9 Carpenter's Place, and they had often seen the man coming and going. He had a wife, a brown-eyed woman in her thirties, and a little boy perhaps four years old who was given to violent tantrums, so much so that his mother had often scolded him, "You naughty cross child."

Eight days later, having followed the scent as far as it would take him, yet without having found his sister, William Gay made his way to Paddington Work House, where he applied to Mr. Thornton, the parish warden, for permission to see the head of the dead woman, which had been preserved in a jar of spirits.

---

* Mr. and Mrs. Davis were themselves mystified by Hannah Brown's abrupt disappearance; and their daughter, Hannah, called on Mrs. Blanchard in Goodge Street to inquire after her. But the Davises did not suspect foul play; they thought rather that Hannah "was ashamed to come, on account of her great disappointment in not being married."

CHAPTER SIX

Furies

There are creative agencies in every part of human nature, of which the thousandth part could never be revealed in one life.

—*De Quincey*

I t is the impotence of our senses that deceives, saves us— conceals from us the abysses that lie hidden all around us, in the souls of others. But for that, a walk down a crowded street would show us things which "might appall the divil." The man who, on Christmas Eve, 1836, made his way to Camberwell Green with a parcel wrapped in a handkerchief was in outward aspect unremarkable; yet inwardly he was in the grip of Melinoë, the "black one" who imposes on mortals their just burden of nightmare.

At Camberwell Green, the man got into one of the new horse-drawn omnibuses that had recently begun to ply the streets of the metropolis. It took him north into Southwark, over London Bridge, and down Fish Street Hill past Sir Christopher Wren's Monument, a memorial of the fire of 1666 much favored, in the early nineteenth century, by those in contemplation of suicide.

The man alighted at Gracechurch Street and went up, in the teeth of a north wind, to Cornhill. A Mile End omnibus was going by; he got aboard and rode it down Leadenhall Street into Whitechapel. At Mile End Road, Stepney, he got off and, going past the alms houses and the Jews' Burying Ground, came to the Regent's Canal, where he turned off into the blackness.

The next day was Christmas Day. London awoke to a heavy fall of snow. The man made his way up Camberwell Road to a house in Portland Street, Walworth. The landlord, Mr. Wignal, had recently let the back parlor to a woman and her young child; the man and the woman dined there on boiled turnips and a scrag of mutton. When, after midnight, the man walked back to Camberwell, it was no longer snowing, but the mercury had dropped to twenty-five degrees. In Carpenter's Place, he took a latchkey from his pocket and let himself into No. 6.

——◆——

The "Babel din" of the city was blunted by the snow. There was "such a silence in it," said Thomas Carlyle, who had at last submitted himself to the metropolis. Many persons were drunk, and the sober few, "not the fifth part of the usual number," went "tripping along muffled in cloaks, with blue noses."

Carlyle was at work, that winter, on his book *The French Revolution*, and murder was much on his mind. How to fathom the slaughterous abysses into which France had descended in those years theoretically consecrated to *liberté, égalité,* and *fraternité?* Certainly not by emulating the historians of the previous age, the urbane, polished, ironical style of Gibbon and Voltaire. No, to interpret the fever-frenzy of France in her killing-time, he must forge a new style, as broken and obscure as Gibbon's is lucid and elegant. A new idiom, too, he must have. He could hardly make his reader comprehend the convulsions of Paris by regurgitating the commonplaces of "enlightened Philosophism," the soulless creed, with its desiccated abstractions and "algebraic spectralities," that had made the mischief in the first place. He must find more primal poetries.

Wordsworth told Emerson that he thought Carlyle "sometimes insane." The appearance of madness in his writing is in part the effect of its construction. Its organizing unit is not, as with most writers, the sentence or the paragraph, but the sometimes verb-less, often curiously capitalized phrase, which Carlyle spits out one after the other. Yet it is not merely the eccentric style and imagery of *The French Revolution*—with its "murky-simmering Tophets" and "Night-birds on the wing," its "turbaned Ishmael-ites" and "astrological Chaldeans"—that sets the book apart, but its expressiveness of the bewitchments under which men commit appalling acts. Carlyle's revolutionists dance their death-dances under the influence of so many sorcerers' spells; he paints motive and psychological impulse, not in the eighteenth-century language of reason and common sense, but with symbols lifted from archaic demonologies and defunct *grimoires*. *The French Revolution* swims with Maenads, Syrens, Gorgons, each apparently "fabulous," yet each a mimic sign embodying (Carlyle supposes) some truth of our nature not to be articulated in a vulgar commonplace tongue.* Quite as much as De Quincey, his rival for murder's laureateship, he finds the secret springs of wickedness in those places in the mind where reason's writ does not run.

———•———

---

* This was a Romantic commonplace. "Gorgons, and Hydras, and Chimeras dire—stories of Celæno and the Harpies—may reproduce themselves in the brain of superstition," says Lamb in his essay "Witches, and Other Night Fears," "but they were there before. They are transcripts, types,—the arche-types are in us, and eternal."

The man came out of the house at 6 Carpenter's Place with another, heavier bundle in his arms. Going up Camberwell Road, he wearied of his burden and called to a passing carrier. Might he place his load on the tailboard of the carrier's cart?

"Certainly," the carrier replied. He offered to take the parcel into the cart itself; but the man demurred and placed it on the tail. He followed the cart to the Elephant and Castle, the "Piccadilly Circus of South London," where the carrier stopped for beer. The man called for porter. He was on the point of drinking it down when he saw a stranger eyeing his parcel.

"What are you about?" he shouted. "Are you going to steal my property?"

The stranger denied it. The man, however, was unnerved, as one assailed by snake-haired furies might well be. He hailed a cab and, putting the bundle beneath the flap, directed the driver to take him across the Thames.

CHAPTER SEVEN

Suspect

A fool's mouth is his destruction, and his lips are
the snare of his soul.

—*Proverbs*

I f William Gay entertained any doubts as to whether the head
in the jar in Paddington Work House was his sister's, the scar
on the ear put them to rest. Many years before, a girl had
pulled an earring out of Hannah's ear and in doing so had torn the
flesh of the lobe.

The parish warden notified the Metropolitan Police, and
Inspector George Feltham of the T Division was assigned the case.
After consulting property records, he identified one James Greenacre of 6 Carpenter's Place, Camberwell, as a suspect and applied to
the magistrates for a warrant. By the evening of Sunday, March 26,
he had traced his man to a house in St. Alban's Street, Kennington
Road, Lambeth. Accompanied by a constable of the L Division,

Feltham reached the house between ten and eleven o'clock. The landlord told them that Greenacre had gone to bed for the night.

Feltham knocked on his door. "Greenacre?"

"Yes, what do you want?"

"I want to speak to you. Open the door."

"Who are you?"

"Never mind that. I want to say something to you."

"Wait a bit till I get the tinder-box and a light."

Feltham did not wait; he lifted the latch of the door, which was not fastened, and went in.

In the dimness he saw a man in his shirt, and laid hold of him by the arm.

"What do you want?"

"I'm an inspector of police," Feltham said, "and hold a warrant for your apprehension on suspicion of having murdered Hannah Brown."

The landlord brought a candle, by the light of which Feltham read the warrant. He then asked Greenacre if he knew Hannah Brown.

"No, I know no Hannah Brown."

"Were you never asked in church to a person of that name?"*

"Yes, I was," Greenacre admitted as he pulled on his stockings.

"Where is she now?"

"I don't know . . . you have no right to ask me these questions."

"I don't mean to ask you any more questions," Feltham said before giving him what in the United States has come to be called a Miranda warning: "and I caution you what you say to me, for whatever you do say to me I shall be obliged to repeat elsewhere."

Greenacre's trousers lay beside the bed. Feltham, going over to search them, saw a woman lying in the bed, partially covered by the bedclothes.

---

* That is, had banns of marriage been published ("asked") by a clergyman inquiring whether any of his flock knew cause or just impediment why Hannah Brown and James Greenacre should not be joined together in holy matrimony.

"What woman is that?"

"Why, that is a woman that comes to sleep with me."

"She must get up also, and dress and go with me." Feltham's eye fell upon the woman's hand. "What is that you have in your hand? Let me see it."

It was a brass "Pinchbeck" watch. Feltham took it from her, and two rings from her fingers besides. "Get up," he said, "for you also must go along with me."

The woman did as she was bade. As she dressed, Feltham saw her slip something into her pocket.

"Stop, what have you got in your pocket?" He searched it and found, among other things, a pair of Cornelian ear-drops and two tickets for articles pawned in a Walworth pawnshop.

Greenacre gestured toward some boxes that stood packed and corded for traveling.

"It's a good job you've come [tonight]," he said to Feltham. "I should have been off to America [tomorrow]."

———•———

The prisoners were conveyed by coach to Paddington Green police station, where they were confined in separate cells. About half past twelve, the night sergeant, Michael Brown, found Greenacre lying on his back on the floor with a silk handkerchief "tied into a noose round his right foot, and the other part of the handkerchief tied round his neck." He had apparently preferred a slow and painful death by strangulation to the ignominy of public trial and execution. When Sergeant Brown cut the handkerchief, Greenacre was "stiff" and "apparently dead." Dr. Girdwood, however, revived him. "I don't thank you for what you have done," Greenacre said afterwards. "I wish to die—damn the man that is afraid to die—I am not."

News of the arrests spread swiftly, and when at noon the next day the prisoners were taken in a coach to Marylebone Police Court, crowds of people lined the streets to see them pass. Greenacre, in a brown greatcoat, put on a brave front. Although he was in pain on account of his neck, he carried himself with much coolness, and it was observed that he steadily met the eyes of those who fixed him with their stares. His paramour and fellow prisoner, Sarah Gale, was more placid still and "seemed quite unconcerned at her situation."

The prisoners were led into the police court and placed at the bar before the magistrates.

CHAPTER EIGHT

A Peculiar Odor

No man truly knoweth himself but he groweth
daily more contemptible in his own eyes.

—*Jeremy Taylor*

M any people have affected, and some few sages have perhaps genuinely felt, indifference at the prospect of their own deaths. But surely Carlyle spoke for the greater number of us when he said that it is a hard thing to die. Were it not, we should feel less interest than we do in the man who knows that the odds are a hundred to one he will be hanged in a fortnight. If the Crown proved its case, James Greenacre would find a halter around his neck before the roses bloomed. Few things bring out a man's character as effectually as the prospect of the hangman's knot. The death-grapple of Greenacre was no exception: it laid bare the truth of his nature and reproduced, in a compressed form, its peculiar moral odor.

He had been born, in 1785, into a family of farmers in Norfolk. Possibly through the agency of a generous stepfather, he had been able to set up, before he was twenty, as a greengrocer in London; in time, he had become the proprietor of a greengrocer's shop in the Kent Road. He had speculated as boldly in real estate and politics as he had in greengrocery. He was, at one time, master of more than a dozen properties in Southwark and Camberwell, and when he was not pushing his business interests south of the Thames he might be found in the White Lion in Wych Street, voicing radical opinions on the great public questions of the day. Such, indeed, was his reputation as a coffee-house politician that he was elected, in 1832, overseer of his parish, that of St. George the Martyr in Southwark.

But like many another man who would brazen his way into eminence, Greenacre courted fortune with borrowed money, and soon enough the bills came due. He attempted to recoup his losses by going into the tea trade, and his method of establishing himself in that market was, to say the least, ingenious. Drawing on the rhetorical skills he had refined in the White Lion, he composed a pamphlet warning his fellow citizens of the evils of spurious teas adulterated with the leaves of the sloe tree or blackthorn. Doubtless many customers were only too happy to purchase their tea from a merchant so devoted to the purity of his merchandise; but just as Greenacre's fortunes seemed likely to mend, the Excise officers seized a quantity of sloe leaves in his shop. A heavy fine was laid upon him "for this fraud upon the public and government."

Unable to pay the fine, Greenacre fled to America, leaving behind him a mass of debts and three dead wives.* In New York he

---

* The first of Greenacre's wives, a girl from Woolwich, died suddenly of what Greenacre called "a putrid sore throat." He next married the daughter an Essex farmer; according to Greenacre, she "died of a brain fever brought on by exerting herself, I believe, riding on horseback, whilst on a visit at her own relations." Fifteen months later he wed Miss Simmonds; she succumbed, by his account, to cholera in 1833, the year he fled to America. None of the deaths, it seems, excited suspicion at the time; but given Greenacre's subsequent history, one would like to know more about them.

attempted to redeem his failures with a washing machine of his own invention. But although he obtained a patent for the device, the venture failed. He took to writing pamphlets in which he set forth his grievances against his persecutors, and he appealed to the citizens of the United States to come to the aid of an "injured Englishman" who had suffered unjustly at the hands of His Majesty's Excise. But the appeal went unanswered and, after being twice imprisoned in New York for libel, he returned to England, where he had been declared a bankrupt. In London he engaged in a new venture, peddling an "amalgamated candy" which, he claimed, had for its principal ingredient a potent herb he had discovered in America, a most effectual remedy for maladies of the throat and chest. At the same time, he continued his exertions as a pamphleteer, publishing an address in which he implored a "generous public" to help him "satisfy all his just debts, and re-establish himself in business again." Oddly enough, this appeal, too, went unanswered.

With the failure of these projects, Greenacre determined on another path to ease and plenty: he would marry a woman of property. The untimely death of the first object of this speculative affection, Hannah Brown, did nothing to diminish his faith in the underlying soundness of his plan, and in January 1837 he placed the following advertisement in *The Times*:

> *Wanted*, a partner, who can command £300 to join the advertiser in a patent to bring forward a new-invented machine, of great public benefit, that is certain of realising an ample reward. Applications by letter only (post-paid), for J. G., at Mr. Bishop's, No. 1, Tudor-place, Tottenham Court-road.

At least one woman answered the notice. On February 4, two days after Hannah Brown's severed legs were found among the willows of Coldharbour Lane, Greenacre replied to the lady. Describing himself as a thirty-eight-year-old widower (in fact he was past

CHAPTER NINE

Sarah Gale

She was sparing of the truth, loved equivocation
and duplicity. . . .

—*D'Alton*

A new age was struggling to be born. It did not yet have a
name, but the figure who was to give it one was about
to make her debut on the world stage. This, however, is
to anticipate, for in April 1837 she was a girl of seventeen living
in seclusion in Kensington Palace. With the coming of the spring,
she and her mother, the Duchess of Kent, resumed their walks in
Kensington Gardens. They were followed, at a respectful distance,
by a detective tasked with keeping an eye on an old man who had
taken to bowing repeatedly to the young lady, and who had named
his cottage in her honor.

Greenacre had but one hope of living to see the dawn of the
Victorian age. He must convince if not the world, at any rate a jury

of his peers that the death of Hannah Brown was an accident—a dreadful one to be sure, but not the sort of thing that justified his being hanged by the neck at Newgate. In his initial examination in Marylebone Police Court, Greenacre offered the first of several accounts he was to give of the circumstances in which Mrs. Brown had paid her debt to eternity. He admitted at once that he knew her, had indeed engaged himself to marry her; but he had sought her hand only because he believed that she could "command at any time three or four hundred pounds." On Christmas Eve he was cruelly undeceived. Mrs. Brown appeared on the doorstep of his house in Camberwell Place that afternoon, somewhat "the worse for liquor." Over tea, he told her he had made "inquiry about her character, and had ascertained that she had been to Smith's tally-shop in Long Acre, and tried to procure silk gowns" in his name. Hannah conceded that she had very little savings; she seems in fact to have been living day to day, hand to mouth. Yet when Greenacre quite naturally expressed displeasure at the deception that she had practiced upon him, she "put on a feigned laugh" and coolly replied that he was as guilty as she. Had he not lied to her about the extent of his own property? The imaginary farm at Hudson's Bay? She "then began to sneer and laugh," Greenacre said, "at the same time rocking herself backwards and forwards in her chair."

This was too much for him; and while she was "on the swing" he impulsively put his foot to the chair. She fell backwards in it to the floor, and the back of her head came with "great violence" against a clump of wood which lay there. This "alarmed me very much," Greenacre said, "and I went round the table and took her by the hand, and kept shaking her, but she appeared entirely gone."

"I deliberated for a short time" and "unfortunately determined on putting her away" in order to "conceal her death." "I thought it might be more safe that way than if I gave an alarm of what had occurred." He did not seek help lest he "should be set down for a murderer"; to dispose of the body secretly was altogether the "safest and most prudent plan."

———•———

Beside the slyness and duplicity of Greenacre, Jack Thurtell, with his naïve ingenuous strength, seems almost noble in his savagery, a Bronze Age brigand. Thurtell's crime—the prosecution of private revenge—has, for the greater part of human history, been held to be perfectly compatible with the strictest honor; and until the day before yesterday the morality of *la vendetta* prevailed in the wilder regions of Europe, and indeed still survives in the gangs of the American city. But the most hardened bandit would not dream of striking a woman, let alone a woman whom he had engaged himself to marry. Greenacre violated this unwritten law. And yet, ignoble though he was, he was not without gallantries of his own; and it is but just to record that he never wavered in his effort to exculpate Sarah Gale of complicity in the death of Mrs. Brown.

Of all the phantoms in Greenacre's little inferno, Sarah Gale is the most obscure. Little is known of her early history, other than that her maiden name was Farr, and that she came from Dorset. On coming up to London, she joined a theatrical troupe, performing under the stage name of Sarah Wiston; but her career as an actress did not prosper, and she fell into prostitution. A man connected with the legal profession kept her for a time; he, however, left her, and she stooped to marry a coachman named Gale, whose child she bore. When the coachman, too, abandoned her, she took Greenacre for a lover.

As the gravity of her position became clearer, she grew more alarmed. "I have nothing to say," she told the magistrates when they asked her about the death of Hannah Brown. "I know nothing about it." There was, however, a good deal of circumstantial evidence to suggest that she knew more about it than she was willing to admit. On the day after Christmas, she had been seen, by the neighbors, at 6 Carpenter's Place "employed with a bucket and mop, as if she were hard at work" cleaning up a mess. A week later, when Greenacre moved his belongings out of Carpenter's

Place, she made what in retrospect was a damning remark. The boxes and trunks had been placed on the cart when Greenacre, who up to that moment had been tremulously anxious, breathed a sigh of relief: "all," he said, was "right," as he should soon be off to America. Unfortunately he said this in the hearing of the man whom he had hired to help him move, an indiscretion which moved Sarah Gale to exclaim, "Ah, now you have done for yourself." A short time later, she pawned two veils belonging to Mrs. Brown in a shop in Walworth.

Greenacre exerted himself to save her. "This female," he told the magistrates, "I perfectly exonerate from having any more knowledge of it than any other person, as she was away from the house. . . . That's all I have to say." He paused for a moment. "Mrs. Brown had eleven sovereigns by her, and a few shillings in silver, and that's a true statement."*

---

* In crime as in other departments of life, the age of chivalry has passed away; Greenacre's steadfast refusal to incriminate his mistress stands in contrast to the conduct of a villain convicted in a more recent case of murder and dismemberment in London. The "jigsaw" killer Stephen Marshall contended that it was not he but his girlfriend Sarah Bush who murdered Jeffrey Howe in March 2009. But the evidence produced by the Crown was overwhelming, and in the midst of his trial in St. Albans Crown Court he withdrew his plea and confessed his guilt.

CHAPTER TEN

Newgate

In my warm blood and canicular days I perceive
I do anticipate the vices of the age; the world to
me is but a dream or mock-shadow, and we are all
therein but pantalones and antics, to my severer
contemplations.

—*Sir Thomas Browne*

So great was the fury of the crowds that gathered each day
outside the Marylebone Police Office that the magistrates
deemed it prudent to remove the prisoners to safer places of
confinement. Greenacre was taken to the New Prison in London's
Clerkenwell parish, Mrs. Gale to Tothill Fields in Westminster,
where the Cathedral now stands. At their final examination in the
New Prison, both prisoners trembled violently. The magistrates
ordered their committal for trial and remanded them to Newgate,
there to await, in its gloomy recesses, their judgment at law.

Monday April 10, 1837, was the day fixed for the trial. It was a bleak, cold day; Greenacre, dressed in a blue coat and dark waistcoat, was led from his cell to the Sessions House, better known as the Old Bailey, the seat of the Central Criminal Court. He went by way of the narrow passage known as Birdcage Walk, so called because it was roofed with an iron grate. Beneath its flagstones, the corpses of executed felons moldered in quicklime; their initials were carved on its walls.

Greenacre was conducted up a narrow staircase to the Old Court, a dingy, oak-paneled chamber adorned with Doric pilasters. Through the windows, Newgate's windowless south wall was visible, soot-blackened and megalithic. Greenacre was put into the dock; so also was Sarah Gale.

At ten o'clock, the judges came in. The most senior of them was Sir Nicholas Conyngham Tindal, Lord Chief Justice of Common Pleas, one of the two principal common-law courts in the Kingdom, the other being the King's Bench. He was followed by Mr. Justice Coltman, a "truly right-minded judge" and "the perfection of good sense." The most junior of the three judges, Mr. Justice Coleridge, was a nephew of the poet.

The jury was sworn, and the prisoners, having been arraigned on the indictment, were placed at the bar to answer the charges against them. Both pleaded not guilty.

John Adolphus opened the case for the Crown.[*] He was, at sixty-eight, among the foremost trial lawyers in England, the "father of the Old Bailey bar." He had the voice of a great advocate, "clear, mellow, and flexible," but not the pride of vocation which makes a barrister not merely successful but happy in his work. The incessant labor of eliciting the truth of the squalid acts committed by the more vicious reprobates of the metropolis had worn away the finer edges of his temper and character; and it seemed to some, seemed

---

[*] Born in 1768; admitted to the Inner Temple in 1807 and called to the Bar in the same year; died in 1845.

perhaps even to himself, that he had failed to live up to the promise he had shown, many years before, as a rising young lawyer, author, and politician. It was the tragedy of John Adolphus to have been, in the words of a contemporary, *"nearly* a great man."

As Greenacre himself did not deny that he had killed Hannah Brown—he contended that her death was an accident—the principal task of the Crown lawyers was to persuade the jury to convict him of capital murder, which was punishable by hanging, and not the lesser crime of aggravated manslaughter, which would spare him the gallows. The testimony of Dr. Girdwood proved decisive. The fact that Mrs. Brown had sustained "an extraordinary black eye," he testified, together with the fact that the skin around the eye showed a discoloration associated with an *ecchymosis,* or forcing out of the blood, could only mean that the blow she received had been "inflicted during life." Also, such an injury to the front of the face was quite obviously inconsistent with Greenacre's account of Mrs. Brown falling backwards in her chair and hitting the back of her head against a clump of wood; nor could the wound, being not a postmortem one, have been caused by the grappling hook which was used to fish the head out of the canal. Moreover, Mrs. Brown's throat had been cut, and the "bloodless state of the arteries" of her head proved that this injury, too, had occurred while she was still alive, or only very shortly after her death.

———•———

The jurors deliberated for less than a quarter of an hour before finding Greenacre guilty of felony murder and Mrs. Gale guilty of being an accessory after the fact. Greenacre, from pride, vanity, or a secret sense of the real justice of the verdict, displayed no emotion. His expression, one observer said, remained unaltered, and he leaned back in his chair as though he were "perfectly indifferent" to the decision. Mrs. Gale seemed as one in a trance or a stupor and appeared "almost unconscious of what was passing around her."

A moment later, loud cheers were heard: the crowd in the street had learned of the verdicts. The next day, the Recorder of the City, Charles Ewan Law,* pronounced sentence upon the prisoners: death on the gallows for Greenacre, "transportation beyond the sea" for Mrs. Gale, which in effect meant that she would spend the rest of her days in New South Wales in Australia.

---

* Born in 1792, second son of Lord Ellenborough; St. John's College, Cambridge; called to the Bar in 1817; took silk in Michaelmas Term 1829; Recorder of the City from 1833; Tory M.P. for Cambridge from 1835; died in Eaton Place in 1850.

CHAPTER ELEVEN

A Philosophical Murderer

One thing only do I teach, O monks,
sorrow, and the uprooting of sorrow.

—*Buddha*

Greenacre was conducted not, as was customary following capital convictions, to one of the condemned cells in Newgate, but to the cell he had previously occupied in the prison, where he could be more strictly watched lest he make another attempt on his own life. He was obliged to wear a strait-jacket, an inconvenience he complained of to the Home Secretary, Lord John Russell, who, however, declined to act in the matter. The authorities were, indeed, never more zealous to keep Greenacre alive than now when he was legally dead. For the sentence of death is not only "the most terrible and highest judgment" in the English statute book, Blackstone says in the *Commentaries on the Laws of England*, it is a declaration that the condemned man, "by an anticipation of his punishment," is "already dead in law." He is called "attaint, *attinctus*, stained or blackened" and, being no longer "fit to live upon the earth," is "to be exterminated as a monster and a bane to human society."

The Recorder of the City, meanwhile, communicated Greenacre's sentence to the King, and upon His Majesty's declining to exercise the royal prerogative of mercy, the death day was fixed. Greenacre was to be hanged on the second of May; he had little more than a fortnight left to live. He said that he "cared nothing for death," but he "shuddered at the thought of quitting life with the brand upon him of a willful murderer." Putting pen to paper, he set out, yet again, to prove that the death of Mrs. Brown was an accident. He labored for several days at the task; but none of his drafts pleased him, and in the end he consigned them to the flames.

He did, however, confess to the sheriffs that in one respect his previous accounts of Mrs. Brown's death were false. In the latest version, he told how, after he and Hannah had tea on Christmas Eve, she rose to wash the tea things. The sun had set; the room was lit only by candlelight. While Hannah was at the sink, she continued to discuss her property, or lack thereof, with her fiancé. He, for his part, became "enraged at the deception which she had practised on him" and, seizing a rolling pin, struck her in the eye. She fell to the ground; and he was "shocked," he said, to find her "insensible, and apparently dead." He also told the sheriffs that, contrary to the reports in the newspapers, he had placed the sack containing Mrs. Brown's trunk behind the paving-stone in the Canterbury Villas in broad daylight, for "he conceived that he underwent less risk in pursuing his operations thus openly, than in endeavouring to conceal them under the shades of night." As for the handkerchief in which he had concealed her head when he took it on the omnibus, he had burned it; the blood on the floor of his house he had wiped up with flannel cloths, which he had afterwards put down the privy.

———•———

It is not every murderer who obtains a place in the immortal pages of philosophy. Yet by a singular chance, James Greenacre did. No less a philosopher than Arthur Schopenhauer fingered him as a man who through intense suffering had attained the highest wisdom.

At the heart of Schopenhauer's book *The World as Will and Representation* is the idea that, although we are all acquainted with misery in life, comparatively few of us perceive its real nature and extent. We are saved, or rather damned, by our egotism or what Schopenhauer calls the "will to live"—that part of our being which would have us elbow our way to the front of every line under the (quite erroneous) impression that whatever is to be found at the front of it is worth elbowing for. All the cruelty and torment of the world, Schopenhauer says, is a product of this will to live: it creates the illusions—power, riches, sex, fame—we pursue in the belief that their attainment will make us happy. A fantasy, Schopenhauer says. For the will (being insatiable, desire-mad, rapacious of gain, reeking of the "more-having" the Greeks call *pleonexia*) is not only incapable of lasting contentment, it is also delusional and unable to comprehend that the "pain which is essential" to life cannot be thrown off. Our "ceaseless efforts to banish suffering" accomplish "no more than to make it change its form"; and if we succeed, at last, in removing pain in one of its forms, "it immediately assumes a thousand others. . . ."

It is at first sight curious that Schopenhauer should have numbered Greenacre among the elect who perceived the master-truth of *The World as Will and Representation*. Greenacre possessed a limited intelligence, precisely the kind Schopenhauer associated with fools who submit with bovine docility to the stupidities of life. Nor had Greenacre improved the weakness of his understanding through study and reflection. He had not so much as dipped into the thought of Schopenhauer's philosophic heroes, the Indian sages, who looked with pity on those entangled in the delusions of a sensual world which is but a charlatanry of *Mâyâ*, a "summoned enchantment, an inconstant appearance without true being, like an optical illusion or a dream." Nor was Greenacre better versed in the teachings of Buddha, who sorrowed to see men struggling under the grievous burdens of worldly existence when they would do better to seek Nirvana, the "negation of the world." As for another of Schopenhauer's favorites, the French mystic Madame de Guyon, who trod the path of "renunciation, of interior death, of self-annihilation," it is unlikely that Greenacre had ever heard of her.

Schopenhauer nevertheless forgave Greenacre his stupidity and his cruelty: he was for him the idiot savant who proved that even imbeciles could be brought to discern the truth of his philosophy, that nothing can "be given as the end of our existence but the knowledge that we had better not be."

———•———

Schopenhauer was in his fiftieth year when Greenacre was brought to trial. The patrimony bequeathed him by his father, a Danzig merchant prince, afforded him the leisure and liberty of a philosopher, and as a young man he saw more of the great world than is commonly the case with German intellectuals. Before his departure for Italy, Goethe gave him a letter of introduction to Lord Byron, and in Venice he caught a glimpse of the poet in his gondola. But on observing how his mistress swooned at the sight of the beautiful *milord*, he chose not to risk an acquaintance that might end in his own cuckoldry, or so the perhaps-apocryphal story goes. He later regretted this and thought it remarkable that the three great Romantic pessimists should have been in Italy at the same moment—"Byron, Leopardi, and myself! And yet not one of us has made the acquaintance of the other."

Given his low opinion of the human race, Schopenhauer ought perhaps to have foreseen that it would fail to interest itself in what

Nietzsche called the "cadaverous perfume" of his philosophy; but when the first edition of *The World as Will and Representation* fell dead-born from the press, he suffered quite as much as less philosophic authors do when their books fail. He continued, however, to cherish a paternal affection for the stillborn volume, and he was diligent in the collection of fresh proofs of the soundness of its theories. His father had made it a practice to look at the French and English newspapers as well as the German ones each day, and during much of his life Schopenhauer did the same. He was drawn especially to accounts of executions, the gallows being for him "a place of quite peculiar revelations," a "watch-tower from which the man who even then retains his presence of mind obtains a wider, clearer outlook into eternity than most philosophers over the paragraphs of their rational psychology and theology."

More to the point, the gallows was a place of acute suffering. Dostoevsky, who as a young man had been about to be hanged when the Tsar's reprieve came, spoke from experience of the terror felt by a man who knows, to a virtual certainty, that he will be dead within the hour.* What fascinated Schopenhauer about such cases was the power of this anguish to annihilate the will to live, and to force even the coarsely animal soul to see life for what, in Schopenhauer's view, it really is—a Gothic horror, and a painful mistake. As evidence of such gallows conversions, he pointed (in the second, enlarged edition of *The World as Will and Representation*, which appeared in 1844) to the extinction of personality which took place in one Mary Cooney, a servant girl hanged at Gallows

---

* In Dostoevsky's *The Idiot*, Prince Myshkin argues that the death penalty "is a punishment incomparably worse than the crime itself. Murder by legal sentence is immeasurably more terrible than murder by brigands. Anyone murdered by brigands, whose throat is cut at night in a wood, or something of that sort, must surely hope to escape till the very last minute. . . . But in the other case all that last hope, which makes dying ten times as easy, is taken away for certain. There is the sentence, and the whole awful torture lies in the fact that there is certainly no escape, and there is no torture in the world more terrible."

Green, Limerick, in 1837 for the murder of an old widow lady. The newspapers reported that, as she stood on the scaffold waiting to die, she "kissed the rope which encircled her neck," a gesture Schopenhauer interpreted as the outward sign of her inward longing for the grace of non-being.

"Still more remarkable," he said, were the sentiments attributed to "the well-known murderer, Greenacre." He made much of Greenacre's refusal to accept the suggestion of the Newgate chaplain, the Rev. Dr. Horace Cotton, that he "pray for forgiveness through the mediation of Jesus Christ." Greenacre replied that "forgiveness through the mediation of Christ was a matter of opinion; for his part, he believed that in the sight of the highest Being, a Mohammedan was as good as a Christian and had just as much claim to salvation." Ever since his imprisonment, he said, he had directed his attention "to theological subjects," and he had become convinced not only of the comparative insignificance of sectarian dogmas, but of the supreme grace conferred by the halter. The gallows, he declared, was "a passport to heaven"—a proposition to which the Rev. Dr. Cotton, who was fond of expatiating on the hellfire in which his parishioners would be burnt if they rejected his ministrations, could by no means assent.

Schopenhauer believed that it was just this indifference to religious orthodoxy that proved Greenacre's words to be the image of his chastened soul. He spoke not under the "fanatical delusion" of received opinion and conventional wisdom, but from "individual immediate knowledge." His words were those of a man standing in the "presence of a violent and certain death," and the very horribleness of his position was for Schopenhauer the guarantor of his candor.

Undoubtedly, Greenacre spoke the words to which Schopenhauer attached such significance from the depths of a pit. His last hours were upon him. The only question is whether, in the brief interval of life that remained to him, he was quite so entirely liberated from the world as the philosopher supposed.

CHAPTER TWELVE

The Gallows

Not merely philosophy but also the arts work at
bottom towards the solution of the problem of
existence: "What is life?"

—*Schopenhauer*

On the eve of his death, Greenacre slept soundly. When, at four o'clock on the morning of May 2, he rose from his bed, workmen were already engaged in assembling, in front of the Debtors' Door, the scaffold on which he was in a few hours to die.

He dressed, wrote several letters, and breakfasted; afterwards he was seen to weep. At a quarter to eight, the tenor bell in the bell-tower of St. Sepulchre-without-Newgate began to toll; he was by this time visibly agitated.

The mild morning was full of the promise of the spring, of the renewal of the earth; but the immense crowd that was by this time gathered outside the prison was transfixed by the thought not of life but of death. Some of the spectators had come as early as the night before and had slept under the stars; not a few were in a "state of beastly intoxication, laughing, singing, dancing, fighting." A young Glasgow merchant in London on business was appalled by the sight of the "smoking, drinking, laughing vagabonds," revels not unlike those with which primitive peoples propitiated their vegetation gods.

Greenacre, in his double character as an atavistic scapegoat and a symbol of the rational retribution of the law, submitted without complaint to having his hands tied and his arms pinioned with leather straps.* Afterwards, a horrible howling was heard; it betokened the appearance, on the scaffold, of the hangman, Calcraft. The sight of this man fingering the tools of his trade drove the crowd to a new height of delirious ecstasy.

The procession to the gallows commenced. The constables, sheriffs, and other responsible officers passed through the Debtors' Door to a covered platform. The sheriffs took their places beside the two flights of steps that led to the scaffold: the other dignitaries proceeded to the viewing galleries that had been arranged about three of the scaffold's sides.

The death of a man on the gallows is a rare public edition of a fact which, like the other great biological acts of birth and copulation, is generally hid under so many decent veils. We have innumerable

---

* It was the indignity of the binding of the hands that is said to have particularly disconcerted Louis XVI on the day of his death. His confessor, it is said, implored him to submit to this last humiliation in the manner of his divine model, and afterwards exhorted him with the famous words *"Fils de saint Louis, montez au ciel"* ("Son of St. Louis, ascend to heaven").

accounts of natural deaths in private rooms; but as a rule they have been sanitized, and in reading them one feels a little in the dark as to what actually happened. The dying person, in these deathbed scenes, is apt to be suspiciously calm, wise, and even epigrammatic; he says something profound, like the dying Goethe ("*Mehr Licht!*") or witty, like the dying Voltaire, who, when asked whether he rejected Satan and all his works, replied, "This is no time to be making enemies."

A public execution is a very different kettle of fish; there is no question of an hygienic suppression of grotesquerie; indeed, the more nauseating the detail, the more eagerly it is seized upon and treasured up. A dozen witnesses punctiliously record every word that drops from the soon-to-be-dead man's lips; and after his fall, there is no twitch or shudder of his dangling body that is not scrupulously set down for the edification of posterity.

Even so, there is a barrier. The gallows is a stage, and those who tread it are conscious of playing a part. They will not, of course, live to read the critics' appraisals of their performances; but whether from pride, vanity, or the decorous shyness that shrinks from making a scene (even though it be the scene of one's death), the gallows-goer is as a rule careful to observe the proper forms. Miss Blandy, sentenced to die at Oxford for having poisoned her father, went up the black-draped ladder with a wonderful propriety and, what was still more meritorious, a consciousness of what was due to her feminine dignity. "Gentlemen," she said to those who were about to kill her, "pray do not for the sake of decency hang me too high." Jack Sheppard, the notorious burglar, was praised for having behaved "very gravely"* in his last moments, while the robber John Waistcott was admired for the coolness of the self-possession he showed at the end of his

---

* No pun, I think, was intended. See *Select Trials at the Sessions-House of the Old-Bailey, for Murder, Robberies, Rapes, Sodomy, Coining, Frauds, Bigamy, and Other Offences* (London: J. Applebee, 1742), II, 146.

tether: "The dog died game," the dandy George "Gilly" Williams told his friend George Selwyn.* Jack Thurtell himself, who for a time had been universally reviled as a swine in human form, bore himself so beautifully at his trial and on the gibbet that his crime, in the popular imagination, lost half its grossness, and he became something of a folk hero.

For the condemned man who courted public favor, there was an established ritual to be enacted on the day of his dying. He was the hero of a tragedy in comic form; he was expected to make his way to the fatal tree with a superb nonchalance. His progress from Newgate to Tyburn, where until 1783 London's capital convicts were hanged, had a carnival air. He was showered with nosegays, and at an alehouse near St. Giles was presented with a flagon of ale, the "Giles Bowl," which he dutifully drank down.

It was a grave breach of etiquette if the bravo let the comic mask slip, even for a moment, to reveal the soul that cowered beneath.** As his death-day drew nigh, the highwayman Paul Lewis found himself unable to sustain the pose of bluster and swagger he had previously exhibited before the world: he "became as abject as before he appeared

---

* It is to be regretted that Selwyn never wrote a study of men under sentence of death. He was, his friend "Horry" Walpole said, one of those "whose passion it is to see coffins and corpses, and executions." When a prior engagement obliged Selwyn to miss a hanging, he relied on friends to supply him with the lurid details. "So eager," it is said, "was he to miss no sight worth seeing, that he went purposely to Paris to witness the torture of the unhappy Damiens," who had made an attempt on Louis XV. "On the day of the execution, he mingled with the crowd in a plain undress suit and bob wig; when a French nobleman, observing the deep interest he took in the scene, and imagining from the plainness of his attire that he must be a person in the humbler ranks of life, resolved that he must infallibly be a hangman." "Eh bien, monsieur," he said to Selwyn. "You have come to see the spectacle?" "Oui, monsieur." "You are bourreau [executioner]?" "Non, monsieur, I have not that honour; I am but an amateur."

** It is not an easy thing to conceal the soul in such circumstances. A visitor who saw Joseph Wall, the former governor of Gorée, in Newgate on the morning of his execution said that he "was death's counterfeit, tall, shrivelled, and pale; and his soul shot out so piercingly through the portholes of his head, that the first glance of him nearly petrified me."

hardened," and was generally regarded as a disgrace to his profession. Yet it is perhaps only in cases like Lewis's, when the nerves fail, that we gain some faint insight into what the last moments must really be like. This is why the unconcealed terror of Madame du Barry, the former mistress of Louis XV who was guillotined in 1793, is so much more revealing than the decorous and theatrical exits. Her eyes were "bathed in tears"; she uttered piteous shrieks; the words she spoke to Sanson, the executioner, before the blade fell were long to haunt Dostoevsky. *"Encore un moment, Monsieur le Bourreau, un petit moment."* "Just a moment, Mr. Executioner, just a small moment."

CHAPTER THIRTEEN

The Mercy of Gravity

We was havin a kevarten wen Bill he says, says he,
"Tomorrow is the hanging-match; let us go and see."
I was game for anything: off we set that night;
Ha! the jolly time we spent until the morning light.

'Neath the timbers whereupon the convict was to die,—
(And ugly black the gallows looked atween us and the sky)—
More than thirty thousand of us shouted, yelled, and sung,
Chaffin about murder, and going to be hung.

—*Punch* (1849)

Sometime after eight o'clock, Greenacre came through the Debtors' Door. The crowd had worked itself up into a pitch of hatred such as few mortals could encounter without fear.

One witness says that Greenacre "was totally unmanned" by the animosity directed against him and "was obliged to be supported, or he would have fallen." Another, on the contrary, claims that he showed "great self-possession and strength of nerve." At all events, it is generally agreed that he confessed his apprehension to the tipstaves who attended him: "Don't leave me too long in the concourse and make the rope tight." Some contend that these were the last words he uttered; others say that after he spoke them he requested that his spectacles be given to Sarah Gale. Whether, as Schopenhauer thought, he had by this time lost the will to live is not certain. He may indeed have *hoped* that the gallows would be a passport to paradise, but not, in all likelihood, with quite as much confidence as he had once hoped to get his hands on three or four hundred pounds through the convenient death of an unloved wife. Still, there can be little doubt that in his last moments Greenacre thought extinction on the scaffold a good deal preferable to falling into the clutches of the mob. A special mercy, in its way, the vituperative savagery of the "raff": it seems to have reconciled Greenacre to the impartiality of the rope. The Crown's ultimate executioner, after all, was not Calcraft but gravity, and unlike mobs, gravity does its work dispassionately, is, in the language of Scripture, "no respecter of persons."

———•———

Greenacre crossed the platform and mounted the scaffold. What temper was he in? It is not easy to say. What temper was Louis XVI in when he stepped from his carriage in the Place de la Révolution? "Ten different witnesses will give ten different accounts of it," says Carlyle. "He is in the collision of all tempers; arrived now at the black Mahlstrom and descent of Death: in sorrow, in indignation, in resignation struggling to be resigned." As good a guess as any. As for Greenacre, the historian can only confess his ignorance and surmise that, whatever the nature of his experience, it was beyond words.

CHAPTER FOURTEEN

Sphinxes' Puzzles

> Remember always that the deepest truth, the truest
> of all, is actually "unspeakable," and cannot be
> argued of, dwells far below the region of articulate
> demonstration; it must be felt by trial and indubi-
> table direct experience; then it is known once and
> forever.
>
> —*Thomas Carlyle*

I t was claimed by one observer that the force of the drop liberated one of Greenacre's pinioned arms, and that he instinctively reached for the rope as it tightened round his neck.
Another witness made no mention of a grasping hand but dwelt
instead with distinct pleasure on the spectacle of the suspended
body "quivering in mortal agonies."

What, finally, brought the man to so unfortunate a pass? "The
question of motive in such cases," says an acute scholar of crime,

the Scottish solicitor William Roughead, "is generally a puzzling one, and in the commission of many murders the end to be gained, always inadequate, often remains obscure." It seems likely that Greenacre's original plan was to marry Mrs. Brown, get hold of her money, and use it to sail to America, where he hoped to start a new life in the company of Sarah Gale. That he meditated such a plan would explain why he spoke so distinctly to Hannah Brown's friends of the imaginary farm at Hudson's Bay (of all places), to which he was to return—so he made a point of telling Evan Davis— after Christmas. When, as a consequence of this plan, Hannah came no more to be seen in London, her friends (Greenacre reasoned) would assume that she had, as it were, bought the farm.

The plan was doomed from the start; Hannah Brown was virtually penniless and unable to command the "three or four hundred pounds" Greenacre thought necessary if he were to finance a transatlantic voyage and a new life across the ocean. He was, to say the least, disappointed when he discovered that he had engaged himself to take on the bother of a wife without having secured the blessings of a fortune. And so he hit his prospective bride in the eye with the rolling pin. That the blow was struck in mere unreflecting anger we can, I think, deduce from the fact that, while he had no compunction about consigning Hannah Brown to oblivion, it was not at all convenient for him that she should have reached it on Christmas Eve, 1836. Her removal at that hour was, indeed, peculiarly awkward for him. He could not rely on Hannah's friends to fall for his carefully prepared story that she had gone to America, when he himself was manifestly still in London; and he could not himself get out of London precisely because he lacked the cash he had looked to Hannah's dower-money to supply.*

---

* When, on the night of March 26, Greenacre was arrested in St. Alban's Street, his belongings were found boxed and corded in anticipation of an imminent voyage to America. But it had taken him all of three months to arrange this flight from Great Britain.

There was a second difficulty. His marriage to Hannah Brown was to have taken place on Christmas Day (the day after he killed her). Her friends, the Davises, were to be present at the marriage, and were in fact to give the wedding luncheon. A nuisance, indeed, for Greenacre to have to go round to the Davises on Christmas Eve with a made-up story as to why the wedding was broken off—a fiction that might easily have aroused the Davises' suspicions, though in fact it did not.

There is another mystery that has never been properly cleared up. Was the blow Hannah Brown received from the rolling pin fatal, or likely to have proven fatal? If it was immediately fatal, Greenacre's subsequent conduct is easily explained. More likely, it was not immediately fatal; if it had been, Greenacre would not have needed to undertake the messy business of cutting Mrs. Brown's throat, as the medical evidence and his own confession to the sheriffs make clear that he did. Yet if, in fact, the blow was *not* fatal, why did he proceed from hurting Mrs. Brown to killing her?

The answer is obvious if one considers his predicament. If Hannah Brown had survived and recovered from the blow, Greenacre himself would in all likelihood have been tried, convicted of battery, and transported to New South Wales. Even if he escaped the wrath of the law, he would still have had to undergo the ordeal of trial by gossip. Three wives had died on his watch, and now he had struck a fourth woman, his fiancée, with a rolling pin. Should Mrs. Brown have survived, her friends would soon have known all about his blackguardism. Scandal is sometimes a more effective agent of retribution than statutes; and word would have gotten round that James Greenacre was a gold-digger. We know, from his advertisement in *The Times* in January, that he was still in contemplation of marriage to a rich wife; but with each new revelation of his villainy, his odds of doing so would have grown longer.

It should also be borne in mind that, had Hannah had survived Christmas Eve, Greenacre would still have been troth-plight to her. He would, of course, have had no desire to join himself to a woman whose sole attractiveness, in his eyes, lay in a fortune she did not possess; but should he have broken off the engagement, his jilted fiancée would have had standing to bring an action against him for breach of promise, a common enough proceeding in those days. If she prevailed, she would have been entitled to damages she had sustained as a result of her reliance on his promise to marry her.* Greenacre, bankrupt as he was, would have found even a trifling award to be an unpleasant burden.

Such, perhaps, were the thoughts by which Greenacre was actuated on the night he committed the murder. But a certain obscurity remains. If we look back on the most momentous decisions we have made in our own lives, we are likely to be struck by how many of them were made instinctively, unconsciously—were, we might almost say, made for us. A kind of fatality hangs over our choices; this I suppose is why the great stage tragedies seem to us so true in their account of human chances and human destinies. A small, sordid character like Greenacre's is but a petty thing in comparison to such a work of tragic art as Othello or Oedipus; yet, studied closely, it discloses the same Sphinx's puzzle of madness and unreason, the same horrors, darknesses, inscrutabilities.

---

* Mrs. Brown, it will be remembered, had given up her lodging and sold her mangle—her means of getting a living—in expectation of her marriage.

CHAPTER FIFTEEN

Heroes and Hero-Worship

a broken spirit and a contrite heart
—*Psalm 51*

W hy do men crowd towards the improved-drop at Newgate, eager to catch a sight?" So Thomas Carlyle, who had carefully followed accounts of Greenacre's execution in the newspapers, asked in his essay on Sir Walter Scott, which was published the year after Greenacre's death. They do so, he said, because the "man about to be hanged is in a distinguished situation. Men crowd to such an extent, that Greenacre's is not the only life choked out there."

Carlyle was guilty of an exaggeration, for if it is true that some of those who went to see Greenacre hanged were in danger of being trampled to death, none of them actually perished. But his larger point is not without merit. Carlyle likens the attention we lavish on villains such as Greenacre to the tribute we pay to genuine heroes. Fascination with villains, Carlyle says, is hero-worship gone rancid, corrupted into demon-worship—a phenomenon with which we are sufficiently familiar in our own time. Such fictional villains as Hannibal Lecter and Dexter, with their psychopathic élan, command the heights of popular culture; actual murderers are celebrated for the devil's-party esprit of their characters. Truman Capote's *In Cold Blood* is more properly the gospel of Perry Smith, a book in which the murderer attains practically to sanctification; Manson, Bundy, and Dahmer are very near to being culture heroes. They are the highwaymen of our age; but where the highwaymen of old were honored for their courage and gallantry, their counterparts today are celebrated for their cruelties, depravities, and perversities.

Carlyle thought hero-worship in its purer forms a good thing. "Veneration of great men is perennial in the nature of man," he said in his essay on Scott. "Let hero-worship flourish, we say." Yet when we learn who Carlyle's heroes actually were, we are puzzled. There is in them more than a whiff of Greenacreish contempt for human life. Of Carlyle's two great hero-books, one, the biography of Frederick the Great, is his homage to an architect of the Prussian militarism that culminated in Hitler; it is, indeed, the volume by which Hitler himself was comforted in his last days in the bunker.* The other hero-book, *Oliver Cromwell's Letters and Speeches*, is a panegyric upon a generalissimo whose dictatorship foreshadowed those of Robespierre and Dr. Francia. Anyone who has studied these books without having become intoxicated by them will find it hard to see how Carlyle's supposedly purer forms of heroism differ from the malignant variety embodied by Greenacre, other than that they were on a vastly greater scale.

Yet the reader who lives and breathes for a certain amount of time in the Carlylean atmosphere discovers that Frederick and

---

* Goebbels "told Schwerin von Krosigk how he had recently been reading aloud to the Fuehrer, to solace him in his universal discomfiture. He was reading from his favourite book, Carlyle's *History of Frederick the Great*." See Hugh Trevor-Roper, *The Last Days of Hitler* (New York: Macmillan, 1947), 97.

Oliver are but the excuses for the books, not the books' heroes. The hero is always Carlyle himself. What distinguishes him from the countless other fanciful egotists who have become authors is not merely his superior genius, which gives interest to a subject matter which in lesser hands would be tedious, but the way in which he admitted, when the game was up, that it was all a great sham. Like Greenacre and the other Cagliostro-quacks he delighted to expose, Carlyle, too, had risen by dubious means. Through his writing he had become an Eminent Victorian, one of the literary "lions" who hovered distinguished in glittering lion-*soirées* of the age. But near the end of his life he made an astonishing recantation; his own distinction, he confessed, was hardly less fraudulent than Greenacre's.

———•———

Jane Welsh Carlyle once spoke jestingly of the resemblance between Greenacre and her husband. "I was charmed at your discovering that gallows-expression in Carlyle's picture," she wrote to her cousin, Jeannie Welsh, who had recently seen the artist Samuel Laurence's portrait of the sage of Chelsea. "I have all along been calling it *Greenacre-Carlyle*." The humor was dark. Carlyle was more like Greenacre than he would for a long time have cared to admit. He, too, had a Hannah Brown in his life-tragedy—Jane herself.

Carlyle did not, of course, kill Jane, certainly not in any juridical sense; and although he seems to have abused her bodily on one occasion, the real torment to which he subjected her was not physical. Still, it was severe enough that he came to believe that he had been complicit in a case of soul-murder.

———•———

Carlyle learned from the Rev. Dr. Cotton, the Newgate chaplain, that Greenacre, before he died, told him that "he never had a first love." It is not easy, in our mocking age, to understand the charm the idea of the "first love" had in more sentimental epochs. Eugène Scribe wrote a play called *The First Love*, Turgenev a novella. But the concept is much older than the nineteenth century, is at least as old as Plato, who in the dialogue *Lysis* spoke of the "first beloved"—the *proton philon*—who is the source and origin "of all friendship between human beings." It is "because of our general love for this ultimate object of desire," Plato says, that we are able to "love any individual thing." Indeed, Kierkegaard wrote in *Either/ Or*, our "first love" is the key with which we unlock the secret of our "true love." When Greenacre told the Rev. Dr. Cotton that he never had a "first love," he was, in the idiom of the age, admitting that he had never loved at all.

Leigh Hunt, when Carlyle told him the story, said that Green-acre "was more to be pitied than condemned" for his stunted affections. Carlyle gruffly shook his head: it was, he thought, but another reason to hang him. Their difference of opinion antici-pates the modern debate between Whig liberals, who believe that in judging criminals we should take into account their sufferings and hardships—their loveless childhoods, their poverty, their addictions, their psychological infirmities—and Tory conserva-tives, who regard such excuse-making as the overthrow of all reasonable notions of personal responsibility. But what is most interesting about the exchange is the light it sheds on Carlyle's willingness to condemn Greenacre for a defect of sensibility under which he himself suffered. For Carlyle, too, never had a "first" or "true" love, unless it was his mother.* He was, Jane Carlyle's friend Geraldine Jewsbury told Carlyle's biographer, James Anthony Froude, "one of those persons who ought never

---

* After his father's death, he expressed his love for him in a eulogy that was after-wards published in the *Reminiscences*; and he regretted that he had given the old man so little while he was alive, there having been something "earthly, harsh, sinful" in their relation. "Thou who wouldst give," he wrote, "give quickly. In the grave thy loved one can receive no kindness." But Carlyle could not profit from his own advice; his love-gifts were as a rule posthumous and literary.

to have married." What she meant, in the narrowest sense, is that he was sexually impotent. Whether Miss Jewsbury was right in her supposition is a matter of controversy; but at all events the physical defect, assuming Carlyle suffered from it, was not in itself, insofar as the power of loving was concerned, an insurmountable obstacle. An entirely sexless person, or an avowed celibate, may be, indeed often is, capable of the tenderest devotion. And sexually unexceptional people may, like Greenacre himself, be heartless and cruel. The difficulty in Carlyle's case was that impotence, or some other secret shame or debility, seems to have exacerbated a temper naturally morose.* Except in his relation to his mother, mere loving kindness was dormant in him, and where his wife was concerned, he did not try very hard to awaken it. Rather than acknowledge his weakness and appeal to Jane's compassion, he allowed the wound to fester. It poisoned his life and hers; it poisoned their marriage; by a sad irony, it poisoned the books, disfigured as they are by hate, to which he sacrificed her.**

The intellectual gulf between Carlyle, the world-historic genius, and Greenacre, the small-witted felon, is immeasurably great: the moral one much less so. In the end, however, Carlyle is the nobler of the two. Nobler, not on account of his immensely higher powers of intellect—intellect in itself being neither good nor bad—but in his revulsion at his own hypocrisy. During his lifetime, only a very few people knew anything of his secret faults and failures; as a Victorian public man, he was ranged among the Good and Great

---

* In an essay published after his death as *My Relations with Carlyle*, Froude drew attention to an entry Carlyle made in his journal in which he said "that there was a secret connected with him unknown to his closet friends, that no one knew and know one would know it, and that without a knowledge of it no true biography of him was possible."

** Of course it is easy to exaggerate Jane's victimhood. She bore no resemblance to that conventional figure, the meek, long-sufferering Victorian wallflower of a wife. On the contrary, she had, as Gertrude Himmelfarb has observed, "trenchant opinions" of her own and was "in the habit of expressing them incisively," acts of self-assertion which Carlyle himself encouraged.

and was honored as a prophet and a sage. If it had not been for his willingness to let the truth be known, the world might never have known it.

After Jane Carlyle's death in 1866, he shut himself up in their house in Cheyne Row with her diaries and papers. For the first time, Froude said, Carlyle "was compelled to look himself in the face, and to see what his faults had been." He saw that he had made Jane "entirely miserable; that she had sacrificed her life to him; and that he had made a wretched return for her devotion." Her small fortune had, before his attainment of fame, afforded him the shelter of Craigenputtock, where he composed *Sartor Resartus*; and later, in Cheyne Row, she had ministered to all his whims. But if on occasion he expressed gratitude for this devotion, he more often took it for granted, and even conducted, much to Jane's astonishment and mortification, a platonic flirtation with a woman of fashion, Lady Harriet Baring, afterward Lady Ashburton.

With Jane safely in the grave, Carlyle set out to make amends, assembling a memoir in which he inserted testimonies to his cruelties. Not least of these was an instance of physical abuse which Jane described in her diary: "The chief interest of today," she wrote in the entry for June 26, 1856, "expressed in bluemarks on my wrists!"* Whether Jane was much hurt physically was not, for Victorians, and perhaps not even for us, the point; the point was that the man had dared to lay hands on her at all, however great the provocation.

In going through the papers Carlyle left him, Froude said that for the first time he "realised what a tragedy the life in Cheyne Row had been—a tragedy as stern and real as the story of Œdipus."

---

* In preparing his life of Carlyle, Froude asked Jane's friend Miss Jewsbury if she remembered the "bluemarks." She remembered them "only too well." The marks, she said, "were made by personal violence," inflicted on Jane by her husband. It was said in Carlyle's defense, although not, so far as I know, by Carlyle himself, that Jane was an inordinately provoking woman; this, of course, was what Greenacre, in self-extenuation, said of Mrs. Brown.

What redeems him is the way he repented of his faults. Through the agency of Froude, he admitted that he had watched—as though it were no concern of his—as Jane, day after day, offered up her life to his, laid it upon the altar of his genius and his egotism.

To be sure, Carlyle's confession would have been more effectual had he made it while his victim was still alive. Even so, it was a brave thing.* Certainly Greenacre, who was as insensible of remorse as he was proof against pity, never attained to such humility. (How many of us do?) He insisted, to the end, that the tragedy in which he had played the leading part was not his fault; that he was a good man; and that it was all a terrible mistake.

---·---

Nearly an hour passed before Greenacre's body was cut down from the gallows and taken back into Newgate. It was buried, under cover of darkness, in Birdcage Walk. Sarah Gale was in her cell in the prison with her little boy George when her lover was dispatched; she had not been permitted to see him before his execution. In June, about the time Princess Victoria acceded to the throne of England, Sarah and her boy were removed from Newgate to await their transportation to New South Wales. There she lived for more than half a century, dying in 1888; the fate of little George has not transpired.

---

* How interesting that Carlyle, the prophet of the will, should in this instance have embraced self-mortification rather than invoke that familiar maxim of the heroic egotists he admired, "You can't make an omelette without breaking eggs." He did not, by any means, turn Christian, Buddhist, or Schopenhauerist; yet in his atonement for the evil he had done he was closer to the self-abnegationary philosophies than he was to that of, say, Bonaparte, whom he numbered among those heroes deserving of our worship. When asked by Madame de Brienne whether Turenne was justified in burning the Palatinate, Bonaparte replied, "And why not, Madam, if it was necessary to his designs?"

PART THREE

The Butler Didn't Do It: A Murder in Mayfair

Blood hath been shed ere now, i' the olden time,
Ere human statute purg'd the gentle weal;
Ay, and since too, murders have been perform'd
Too terrible for the ear.
                                    —*Shakespeare*

CHAPTER ONE

The House of Russell

What a tragic, treacherous step dame is vulgar
fortune to her children.

—Thomas Carlyle

In May 1840, Lord William Russell was in his seventy-third
year. He had had a great advantage in life; he had never needed
to explain what he was. He was a Russell; a scion of one of those
families which, like the Cavendishes and the Spencers, had long been at
the pinnacle of the Whig aristocracy of England, that polite and skeptical oligarchy which, for many generations, lorded it over the kingdom.

Yet born though he was into the midst of riches and power,
Lord William had, until the night his throat was cut, passed a comparatively uneventful life. His elder brothers, the fifth and sixth
Dukes of Bedford, had lived in the glare of politics and the great
world; but Lord William himself, although he had dutifully sat in
Parliament, had never distinguished himself there. His nerves were
delicate; they "disqualify me," he said, "from expressing myself in

public," and as a politician he had never risen above dilettantism. When the Tory statesman Mr. Canning became Prime Minister, Lord William supported him, though it cost him the wrath of his Whig brethren to do so; his brother the sixth Duke, who thought Mr. Canning a "political rogue and mountebank," was singularly displeased. It would be pleasant to record that Mr. Canning himself was grateful for Lord William's defection; but this was not the case, and he privately dismissed his disciple as "an acknowledged driveller."

It is unlikely that, constituted as he was, Lord William should under any circumstances have had a brilliant public career; but the death, in 1808, of his wife, the Lady Charlotte Anne, *née* Villiers, foreclosed any lingering hopes he might have had of Parliamentary usefulness. They had married in July 1789, three days before the fall of the Bastille; and he had been devotedly attached to her. After he buried her, the shattered widower passed an aimless existence abroad, now at Lausanne, now at Chamonay, now at Florence, now at Rome, degenerating, at last, into a caricature of the absent-minded *milord*, tottering toward his dotage. His eccentricities grew upon him; and after one of his visits to Woburn Abbey in Bedfordshire, the country seat of the Russells, his sister-in-law, the Duchess of Bedford, unsympathetically observed that he "chatters more and more to himself every day."

To mental debilities were soon added physical ones, and the dried-up grandee was at last constrained to pass the greater number of his days in London, in his house at 14 Norfolk Street (it is now called Dunraven Street) in Mayfair. The house was a small one for a lord,* but it was, a contemporary who visited it said, "adequate for his lordship's wants, and beautifully adorned with pictures and china."

---

* Lord William was not a peer of the realm, entitled to sit in the House of Lords; but where the nobility are concerned, the English courteously extend certain of the father's honors to the sons. Lord William's father, Francis, being the eldest son of a peer (the fourth Duke of Bedford), was in courtesy styled Marquess of Tavistock, one of his father's inferior titles. As Francis was in courtesy styled as though he were a peer, so William, his youngest son, was in courtesy styled as though he were the younger son of a peer.

———•———

Tuesday, May 5, 1840, was a day of peculiar gloom; the bright weather with which the month had opened had given way to a sullen sky. Lord William came down to breakfast, as usual, a little before nine o'clock. He was waited on by Mary Hannell, his cook, and François Benjamin Courvoisier, his valet. (Lord William would have pronounced the word *val*-it, not, as the French do, val-*ay*.) Like his house, his lordship's household was, for a man of his station in that age, a small one; in addition to the valet and the cook, he employed a housemaid, a coachman, and a groom. He did not keep a butler, that is, a head-servant of the household; but his valet had in some measure the duties of that office, and in particular had care of Lord William's "plate," the gold and silver ware that adorned his lordship's table. He slept in the servants' quarters on the uppermost story of the house, as did also (in a separate room) the cook and the housemaid. York, the coachman, and Doubleday, the groom, slept in a nearby mews.

After breakfast, Lord William attended to his correspondence, and later in the morning he gave Courvoisier his instructions for the day, one of which would in retrospect appear significant—the order to "send the carriage to fetch his lordship from Brooks's at five o'clock."

Courvoisier was new both to Norfolk Street and to valethood. A twenty-three-year-old Swiss, born at Monte-la-Ville, he had entered Lord William's service five weeks before, bringing with him a good "character" from his previous employer, the banking heir John Minet Fector. Upon his lordship's going out that day, Courvoisier went down to the kitchen for the servants' midday meal. He told the housemaid, Sarah Mancer, that he was apprehensive lest he forget one or another of his lordship's instructions. And what, he wondered, was Brooks's? Miss Mancer said that it was a club. Indeed it was; it was a club in roughly the same way that Buckingham Palace was a house, or St. Peter a fisherman; it was a great citadel of opulent Whiggism.

—•—

After servants' dinner, Courvoisier set out upon his errands, returning to 14 Norfolk Street a little before five o'clock, where he encountered Miss Mancer cleaning one of the passages. He told her he must get his lordship's things out, for his lordship would soon be home and wish to dress for dinner. Miss Mancer gestured toward a stepladder which lay in the passage. Courvoisier had left it there after hanging some pictures.

"Will you take this away?" she asked.

Courvoisier carried the ladder into the small yard at the back of the house and propped it against the wall; it reached almost, though not quite, to the top.

The bell rang at the servants' gate.* It was the upholsterer's man, come to adjust the bell-pull in Lord William's bedroom. While the upholsterer's man was at his task, there was another ring of the bell at the gate; it was Carr, a great friend of Courvoisier's. He sat down to tea with Courvoisier in the kitchen.

At ten past five, York (the coachman) came in. Courvoisier started. "You should have been at Brooks's at five o'clock," he said, "but I forgot to order you; you had better go directly."

York went away at once, in what would prove an unsuccessful attempt to retrieve his lordship from Brooks's.

Courvoisier shrugged off the blunder; he would simply say that his lordship had ordered the carriage for half-past five rather than five.

Miss Mancer said he had "better tell his lordship the truth, and his lordship would forgive him."

---

* This was a gate at the front of the house which gave access, from the street, to the "area," a flight of outdoor stairs that led down to a sunken pavement and the basement door. In those days servants and tradesmen were admitted to the houses of the well-to-do through the basement door: as a rule only rich or gentle people entered through the front—the main or "hall"—door.

"No," Courvoisier said. He "should tell his lordship half-past five o'clock; his lordship was very forgetful, and must pay for his forgetfulness."

Courvoisier took his friend Carr into the pantry, where they were closeted together for some time. It was called the butler's pantry; but as Lord William did not employ a butler, it was *de facto* Courvoisier's own peculiar domain.

CHAPTER TWO

Castles

What is the reason that in all ages the noble's château has been an object of terror? Is it because of
the horrors that were committed there in the old
days? I suppose so.

—*Eugénie de Guérin*

L ike many another Whig grandee, Lord William cherished a
solicitude for the common people. Languid valetudinarian
though he was, he had, on one or two occasions, exerted
himself in the cause of Progress and Humanity with something
that might almost have been mistaken for passion; and he had once
gone so far as to propose, at a reform dinner in Covent Garden, a
toast to the "Sovereignty of the People."

But however egalitarian Lord William was in theory, he was
practically a patrician, and it was only natural that, after an afternoon spent lounging in Brooks's, he should have been vexed that, on

coming down to St. James's Street, he was not met by the familiar sight of York, in wig and powder, seated on the hammer-cloth of his carriage. Clearly he must have a word with his valet. The young man, perhaps on account of his Swiss birth, seemed not to understand that in the England of 1840 democracy was a sentiment, but aristocracy was real.

———•———

Miss Mancer was looking out the window into Norfolk Street when, about twenty minutes to six, she saw Lord William descend from a hackney cab. She went at once to the pantry.

"Courvoisier, his lordship has been obliged to come home in a *cab.*"

A short time later, Lord William summoned Courvoisier to his library and handed him two letters. "You are to take them to the mews for York to deliver by hand," he said, "and you will bring back the dog with you."

Courvoisier took the letters to the kitchen, and he and his friend Carr left the house by the basement door. When, a few minutes later, Courvoisier returned with the dog, he told Miss Mancer that "his lordship seemed angry when he first came in," but "got quite good-tempered after."

Lord William took the dog for a walk in Hyde Park; came back at half past six; and dined alone, "on plate," in the dining room. (To have "no service of plate" was in those days thought a great meanness.) After dinner, Lord William retired to his library.

———•———

Mary Hannell, the cook, washed his lordship's dirty plate and afterwards went to the back yard to fetch cold meat for the servants' supper, bolting the door behind her on her return. She then left the house on a private errand of her own.

It was now near nine o'clock. York came in to take his lordship's dog back to its kennel; Courvoisier and Miss Mancer supped together in the kitchen. They talked of Mary Hannell's having handed in her notice; Courvoisier distinctly sympathized with her desire to get away. He regretted, he said, his own decision to enter Lord William's service, and he complained that he had suffered much ill usage in consequence of his master's senile daftness. He told Miss Mancer how, on a visit to Richmond in April, his lordship had been "very cross and peevish" and had changed his room three times at the inn. Miss Mancer said that there must have been a reason for his lordship's being out of sorts. Courvoisier replied that he had been put out of joint by the loss of a gold locket, one that contained a lock of his late wife's hair.

That Lord William was not a hero to his valet was hardly a revelation to Miss Mancer; Courvoisier had often been heard to mock and disparage his master. "Old Billy," he once said, "was a rum old chap, and if *he* had his money, he would not remain long in England." Miss Mancer told him that his lordship was not so rich as many people supposed—which was true. Lord William was a younger son, and, like many another younger son, he had been sacrificed to the exigencies of primogeniture, with the result that he was frequently embarrassed in his finances.

But Courvoisier was not persuaded. "Ah," he said, "old Billy has money."

———•———

Night had fallen when, about ten o'clock, Mary Hannell returned from her errand. Courvoisier let her in by the front door, which he afterwards locked, bolted, and chained. He then went out by the basement door to fetch some ale from a nearby public house. The servants drank of it together; Mary Hannell and Sarah Mancer would later say that they felt drowsy after having imbibed it.

Miss Mancer went upstairs and, passing the open door of the library, saw Lord William sitting in his chair, reading a book. The flickering light of the candle illuminated the person of her master, but as for his inward personality, and the curious influences that had molded it, these could be read only by the light of the imagination. Lord William was an aristocrat, the recipient of a training that brands the soul as distinctly as the tonsured head distinguishes the devoted monk or the jeweled button the promoted mandarin. The Russell grandeurs, the palaces and pedigrees, were a part of him, lived in him; nor were the Russell horrors—for there *were* horrors—less closely interwoven with the fibers of his being. The founder of the family's fortune, old Sir John Russell, was one of those bold, bad men who under the Tudors engorged themselves through the plunder of the monasteries. He and his heirs erected a great house on the ruins of the Cistercian abbey of Woburn, close by the oak where the last abbot was hanged. Inferior, indeed, in splendor of descent to such houses as De Vere and Talbot, the Russells nevertheless went rapidly up the steps of the peerage, and by the eighteenth century they were invariably ranked among the "Brahmins of the *ton*." But aristocracy, though it is a brilliant flower, yields a bitter fruit. The progress of the Russell magnificos in all the modes of silken selfishness, of gorgeous hauteur, may even now be traced in the canvases of Van Dyke and Kneller, Lely and Gainsborough. But the splendor, though real, was tainted; the blood and bowels of the old abbot were upon it.[*]

———•———

While his lordship read in the library, Sarah Mancer drew the curtains in his bedroom and lighted a fire in the hearth; she also lighted the rushlight on the night-table. Afterwards, she went up

---

[*] Robert Hobbes, the last abbot of Woburn Abbey, was adjudged a traitor, and suffered the penalties of high treason, being hanged, drawn, and quartered.

CHAPTER THREE

A Devilish Pretty Mess

Chaos is come again.

—Shakespeare

The next morning, Sarah Mancer woke, as she usually did, at half past six. Mary Hannell was still in bed when she left the room they shared and knocked on Courvoisier's door: the valet had a habit of oversleeping. Upon coming down the attic stairs, she saw the warming pan lying on the floor near the door to Lord William's bedroom. Courvoisier ought to have taken it down to the kitchen. He had once before left the pan on the landing, and Miss Mancer had pointed out to him that this "was not the proper place to leave it."

On reaching the first floor, Miss Mancer looked into the library. His lordship's writing desk, she saw, was turned around. Four of the drawers were open, and various papers lay scattered about. A screwdriver rested on his lordship's writing chair, and his keys were on the floor. Miss Mancer was not, however, alarmed, for Lord William had on previous occasions left the library in disarray. She passed into the drawing room, opened the shutters, and afterwards descended to the ground floor. There she was startled to find the door to the street fastened only by the latch—it was neither bolted nor chained, as it ought properly to have been. His lordship's blue cloak lay on the floor not far from the door, as did an opera glass, a gold pencil case, a tortoiseshell toothpick case, and a pair of his lordship's spectacles, tipped with silver, together with an assortment of utensils—a silver sugar-dredger, a silver caddy-spoon, the silver top of a salt-dredger, a little cayenne spoon, a silver dish-cover, and the cook's silver thimble.

It was only when Miss Mancer reached the dining room that she allowed mere consternation to give way to horrible imaginings. The drawers and cupboards had been opened and gone through; the candlesticks had been cast on the floor. She ran upstairs and, after telling Mary Hannell what she had seen, went to Courvoisier's door.

"Courvoisier," she said, "do you know of any thing being the matter last night?"

"No," he said, and opened the door. He was dressed in his usual attire, only he was not wearing his coat.

"Do you know what has been the matter last night?"

"No."

"All your silver and things are about."

Miss Mancer thought he looked pale and agitated as he came out of the room clutching his coat. She followed him downstairs. He took up the warming pan and carried it to the dining room, where he set it down. He then went to his pantry; here, too, the cupboard and drawers had been opened and gone through.

"My God," he said, "some one has been robbing us."

"For God's sake, let us go and see where his lordship is," Miss Mancer said.

--·--

They went up to Lord William's bedroom. Courvoisier opened the shutters of a window that overlooked Norfolk Street; Miss Mancer went to the bed, which was obscured, on one side, by the curtains that hung from the canopy. When she came to the open side, she found his lordship in the bed, lying on his back; a towel covered his face.

"My lord, my lord," Miss Mancer cried, and ran screaming out of the room. She went part way up the attic stairs, turned on her heel, and ran down the stairs and out into Norfolk Street. She rang the doorbell at Mr. Latham's house across the way, then crossed the street to Mr. Lloyd's. No sooner did she ring Mr. Lloyd's doorbell than Mr. Latham's butler (his name was Young) came into the street. His lordship, she told him, was murdered, and he should go for the police.

She went back into the house and into the dining room, where she found Courvoisier seated in a chair, writing something on a piece of paper.

"What the devil do you sit here for?" she asked. "Why don't you go out and send for a doctor?"

"I must write to Mr. Russell," he said. William Russell, Lord William's youngest and only surviving son, lived in Belgravia.

York came into the house, followed by Young, Mr. Latham's butler, and together they went up to his lordship's bedroom. There was blood on the bolster, blood on the bedsheet, blood on the towel that covered his lordship's face. Dr. Elsgood, the surgeon, soon appeared; he removed the towel and drew down the bedclothes.

"It was very horrifying," Young remembered. The dead man lay weltering in his own blood; his head was nearly severed from his body.

———•———

Two constables, Baldwin and Rose, were soon upon the doorstep. Sarah Mancer led them to Courvoisier, whom they found seated behind the door of the dining room with his elbows on his knees and his hands covering his face. Baldwin asked him why he did not get up and tender assistance.

Courvoisier made no answer.

The question was repeated, with the same result.

"Rose," Baldwin said to his colleague, "he must know something about this."

The policemen went down to the basement, where they found marks of violence on the door to the back yard. Yet on going up the ladder and inspecting the tops of the walls, they found them covered with a layer of dust apparently undisturbed.

Inspector Tedman had in the meanwhile arrived. Together with Courvoisier and Miss Mancer, he went down to the basement. Courvoisier pointed to the marks on the back door. "Here is where they came in," he said.

They went next to the pantry, where Baldwin and Rose joined them.

Baldwin looked hard at Courvoisier. "You have made a devilish pretty mess of it. You must know all about it."

Courvoisier said nothing.

Miss Mancer said, "Oh dear, my lord is murdered!"

Inspector Tedman asked to be taken to the body.

CHAPTER FOUR

The Queen Conveys Her Sympathy

Thus those celestial fires,
Though seeming mute,
The fallacy of our desires
And all the pride of life confute. . . .

—*Habington*

The news of the murder excited, in places of the highest importance, an interest greater than the habitués of those rarefied realms were accustomed to take in London throat-slashings. In the Palace of Westminster, in Downing Street, in Buckingham Palace itself, there was curiosity, and perhaps even a faint alarm. The Prime Minister, Lord Melbourne, was informed of the crime by Lord William's nephew, Lord John Russell, who, having given up the Home Office, held the portfolio of Colonial Secretary in the Cabinet. Lord Melbourne was not a man to be unduly moved by passing events, however momentous; when he was told that he had been summoned to kiss hands as Prime Minister, he said he thought it "a damned bore." But the murder in Mayfair roused him from his blasé indifference, and he wrote at once to Queen Victoria to deplore what he called a "most shocking event." He went on to inform Her Majesty that the earliest reports suggested that the "persons who did it came for the purpose of robbing the house; they entered by the back of the house and went out at the front door."

———•———

Meanwhile, in 14 Norfolk Street, Courvoisier was conducted to the scene of the crime. He went to the foot of Lord William's bed and, raising his hand, seemed to swoon. It was, he said, a "shocking job." He then fell back into an armchair and lamented the effect the death of his master was likely to have on his prospects in domestic service. "O my God . . . I shall lose my place and 'character' . . . they will think it is me, and I shall never get another place." Romantic Gothicism was quite evidently on the way out; the criminals themselves seemed to sense it. Courvoisier behaved precisely as though he were the Suspected Servant in one of the ironical, drawing-room-comedy murders which Agatha Christie and Dorothy Sayers were later to compose.

In the meanwhile, Inspector Tedman had been looking about. A pompous, self-complacent man, much taken, like Inspector Lestrade in the Holmes stories, with his own sagacity, he was struck both by what he saw and by what he did not see. Conspicuously absent was any instrument capable of causing the injury Lord William had sustained; suicide, therefore, could be ruled out. As conspicuously present were such articles as a silver candlestick, a gold pin, and a Russia leather box, which proved to contain a gold ring. On the dressing table, crested, silver-mounted dressing articles were arranged before the looking glass, while the cupboard near the chimney-piece contained four silver-mounted tobacco pipes and an opera glass.

"It is a very curious thief," Tedman said, "to leave all this valuable property behind."

"It certainly is very strange," Courvoisier replied.

———•———

After being briefed by the Home Secretary, who had gone in person to Norfolk Street, Lord Melbourne wrote again to the Queen. He now called the crime "a most mysterious affair." "The bed was of course deluged with blood," he wrote, "but there were no marks of blood in any other part of the room; so that he had been killed in his bed and by one blow, upon the throat, which had nearly divided his head from his body. The back door of the house was broken open, but there were no traces of persons having approached the door from without. His writing-desk was also broken open and the money taken out, but otherwise little or nothing had been taken away." The Queen, in a letter to the Prime Minister, asked him to convey her sympathy to Lord William's nephew, Lord John Russell.

———•———

The police suspected the servants; but when they searched their bedrooms and personal effects, they found nothing incriminating. In particular, none of the servants' clothing showed the slightest trace of blood. The police were baffled. They had not enough evidence to justify an application for a warrant of arrest; but they nevertheless put the servants under watch, and "care was taken to prevent their having any conference with one another."

CHAPTER FIVE

Servants and Masters

Hail fellow, well met,
All dirty and wet:
Find out, if you can,
Who's master, who's man.

—Swift

All London, the society gossip Charles Greville wrote in his diary, was frightened "out of its wits" by the murder in Mayfair. "Visionary servants and air-drawn razors or carving-knives dance before everybody's imagination, and half the world go to sleep expecting to have their throats cut before morning." Greville was exaggerating; "all London," for him, meant several hundred great households whose inmates relied on large and continuously changing staffs of menials to see them through the day. But however unrepresentative they might have been of London as a whole, Greville's happy few did indeed feel themselves touched in a sensitive place. Top-drawer Englishmen in that age passed the greater part of their lives in close proximity to their servants. From the moment he woke in the morning until the moment he went to bed, a well-to-do English gentleman had a small army of servants at his beck and call; and some of these had access to his person when it was most vulnerable. His servants helped him to bathe and to dress, they brought him his coffee and his tea, they served him his dinner and (when the cloth was withdrawn) brought him his port.

A gentleman knew his familiar servants as well as he knew anyone, and understood them hardly at all. Constantly thrown together with them though he was, he was separated from them by nearly impenetrable barriers of class, education, and money.* Members of the highest classes passed their lives, for the most part, in luxurious ease; if they worked, they devoted themselves to the higher employments of politics or the bar, diplomacy or finance, the church or the army. Members of the servile class labored at their daily drudgery not because they (most of them) found the employment congenial, but because the alternative was beggary and the workhouse. What made their labor still harder, it offered them glimpses of a world of grace, order, and refinement which could never be theirs or their children's.

Yet however strained the master-servant relation was, violence was rare. In 1840, more than a million and a half people were engaged in domestic service in the United Kingdom out of a population of some 26 million. Yet in the three decades between 1810 and 1840, the number of cases in which servants slew their masters could be counted on one hand. The most notorious instance, before

---

* During World War I, a patrician officer, on seeing a group of enlisted men bathing, confessed himself startled to find that they had such white skins. Arthur Balfour, the early-twentieth-century Prime Minister, figured in the eyes of many as the most perfect gentleman of the age. And yet Mr. Balfour is said to have been "wholly unaware of those who minister to his comfort. Of his servants he never knows the least detail, not even their names. . . ."

Lord William's murder, was the Chislehurst murder in 1815. On the night of Sunday, May 30, Mr. Thomson Bonar, a prosperous London merchant, went to bed in his country house in Chislehurst, Kent; his wife, Mrs. Bonar, retired a short time later. The next morning, a servant coming into the master bedroom found Mr. Bonar dead on the floor in a bloody heap. Mrs. Bonar, who had herself been badly beaten, was still alive but expired a short time later. Suspicion fixed on a footman in the household, Philip Nicholson, who afterwards admitted to having been the killer; he was hanged at Pennenden Heath. No satisfactory motive for the murders, however, was ever proved; Nicholson himself said that he had borne no grudge against his master, and he blamed the crime on his having been maddened by drink.

Another notorious instance of servant-on-master crime—if that is what it was—took place in May 1810, when His Royal Highness the Duke of Cumberland, a younger son of George III,[*] was attacked in his bed in St. James's Palace in London. The Duke attempted to flee from his assailant and sustained a superficial wound in the leg. Cornelius Neale, one of the Duke's two valets, heard his master's cry for help and came to his aid. The other valet, Joseph Sellis, did not appear. Search was made, and Sellis was found in his room with his throat cut: the jurors at the inquest returned a verdict of suicide. According to the officially sanctioned theory, Sellis, having attacked his royal master with a saber, fled to his room, and either from remorse or dread of punishment took his own life. But the theory was not universally credited, and the rumor went round that Sellis had been murdered with the Duke's connivance—either because he had remonstrated with his master after finding him making love to Mrs. Sellis, or on account of his having knowledge of his master's secret homosexuality.

---

[*] He was the King's fifth son. In 1837 he ascended the throne of the Kingdom of Hanover, his niece Victoria being debarred from the succession by the Salic Law.

However rare such violence was in fact, the idea of it haunted the imaginations of the patrician classes, much as the vengeful slave haunted the imaginations of the slaveholding classes of the American South and the vindictive serf those of the Russian landowning nobility: in each case, the master class paid for its pre-eminence in the coin of fear and a bad conscience. So great, indeed, was the morbid fascination which the Mayfair murder exercised over the English upper classes that scarcely had the news broken when a long line of carriages was seen wending its way through Norfolk Street. The gentle occupants wanted to have a look at No. 14.

—·—

Two days later, Inspector Pearse took off the skirting boards in Courvoisier's pantry and found a purse, an assortment of gold coins and rings, a silver medal commemorating the Battle of Waterloo, and a £10 Bank of England note. He went at once to Courvoisier, who was being kept under watch in the dining room, and asked him whether he could now look him "in the face."

"I know nothing about them," Courvoisier replied. "I am innocent, my conscience is clear, I never saw the medal before."

Courvoisier's person was then searched, and during this proceeding a gold locket dropped from his breast pocket.

"What's this?" the constable asked.

"Oh, that's a locket—it's mine." Courvoisier took it out of the constable's hand and put it back in his pocket. But when, the next day, the same locket (it proved to be the one Lord William had missed at Richmond) was found concealed between the hearthstones in the kitchen, the valet was taken into custody on suspicion of murder.

CHAPTER SIX

Bloody Linen

But without considering Newgate as no other than human nature with its mask off, which some very shameless writers have done, a thought which no price should purchase me to entertain, I think we may be excused for suspecting, that the splendid palaces of the great are often no other than Newgate with the mask on.

—*Fielding*

Courvoisier was examined by the magistrates in Bow Street and remanded to Tothill Fields Prison in Westminster; but already there were those who were inclined to doubt his guilt, or at least to question whether it could be established beyond a reasonable doubt. "The circumstances of the case are certainly most extraordinary," Charles Greville wrote in his diary, "and though every day produces some fresh cause for suspecting the man Courvoisier, both the fact and the motives are still enveloped in great mystery. People are always ready to jump to a conclusion, and having made up their minds, as most have, that he must have done the deed, they would willingly hang him up at once."

Greville pointed out that there seemed to be "no evidence to convict" the valet "of the actual commission of the deed, and though I believe him to be guilty, I could not, on such a case as there is as yet, find him so if placed on a jury. I am very sceptical about evidence, and know how strangely circumstances sometimes combine to produce appearances of guilt where there may be none."

Others were positively convinced of Courvoisier's innocence. Lady Julia Lockwood, who had previously employed him as second footman in her house, declared herself willing to testify to his good character; Sir George Beaumont, whose butler Courvoisier's uncle was, subscribed £50 toward his defense; and Mr. Fector, his old master, offered to take him back into his service upon his acquittal.

There were, indeed, reasons to doubt the valet's guilt. A quantity of Lord William's silverware, duly catalogued in the most recent inventory, was nowhere to be found in the house. Where had it gone? How had Courvoisier managed to cut a man's throat without getting any blood on his clothes? And if he *had* gotten blood on his clothes, where had the clothes gone? 14 Norfolk Street had been searched from top to bottom, yet no bloody linen was found, with the exception of that in the bed where the murdered man lay and two dirty handkerchiefs with "some spots or marks of blood on them," which were found in Courvoisier's portmanteau. (These, curiously enough, had been overlooked by the police during their initial search of Courvoisier's personal effects.)* It is true that there was no convincing evidence that an intruder had gotten in through any of the three doors to the house; but might there have been another means of entrance?

Courvoisier himself told the police that "it would not look so bad against me had not the property been found in my pantry," and this

---

* It was suggested at the time that the handkerchiefs were placed there by the policemen themselves, desirous of reward money.

was doubtless true. Yet there was no evidence that *he* had hidden the property behind the skirting boards in the pantry; indeed, if he was the murderer, he would have had every motive to conceal the things in any place *other* than his own particular lair.* It was held against him that he fretted about his future in the valet trade when his master lay murdered before him; yet this singular candor was perhaps more suggestive of innocence than of guilt. If he really had killed Lord William, surely he would have had wit enough to feign those feelings of horror and sorrow which the Crown lawyers were afterwards to tax him for failing to display.

Those who doubted Courvoisier's guilt naturally cast a skeptical eye over the two female servants in the household. Was it merely coincidence that on Lord William's last day on earth, Miss Mancer had directed Courvoisier to move the ladder into the yard? Why, on the morning the body was found, had she told Young, Mr. Latham's butler, that his lordship was murdered, when she had fled the bedroom too hastily to have been able to confirm the fact? What was the nature of the errand on which Mary Hannell had gone after supper the night before the killing? If either she or Miss Mancer, acting, perhaps, in concert with an outside party, was at the bottom of the crime, they would naturally have had strong inducements to make it look as though the valet were the villain.

———•———

On remand in Tothill Fields, Courvoisier found himself famous. His name was on countless tongues; newspaper placards blazoned forth the crime of which he stood accused; newsboys cried the latest developments in the case about the streets; and in the plebeian precincts of public houses no less than in the patrician clubs of

---

* It could hardly be doubted that it was Courvoisier who attempted to conceal, between the hearthstones in the kitchen, the locket which he had filched from Lord William at Richmond. But he would have had the same motive to do this even were he guiltless of his lordship's murder.

St. James's Street, wagers were laid as to whether or not the valet would be hanged. Important personages, smitten with jailhouse prurience, asked to be conducted to the cell of the accused, curious to see how a caged animal bore itself in its last extremity. "He is rather ill-looking, with a baddish countenance," Charles Greville wrote after his visit to the prison, "but his manner was calm though dejected, and he was civil and respectful, and not sulky. The people there said he was very restless, and had not slept, and that he was a man of great bodily strength. I did not converse with him."

While Courvoisier awaited the decision of the magistrates in Bow Street, the mortal remains of his late master were removed from Norfolk Street to Chenies, the ancestral manor of the Russells in Buckinghamshire. The cortège was led by two mutes (professional mourners) on horseback, lugubriously dressed in black. Three page boys followed, one of whom bore aloft a plume of black feathers. Next came the principal tenants of the dead man's nephew, His Grace the seventh Duke of Bedford, followed by the pallbearers and a hearse drawn by six horses richly caparisoned. The cortège halted before the church of St. Michael, and the coffin was borne in. Another of the dead man's nephews, Lord Wriothesley Russell, who was also his son-in-law, read the Order for the Burial of the Dead.

> *"I know that my Redeemer liveth. . . . The Lord gave,*
> *and the Lord hath taken away. . . . Blessed be the name*
> *of the Lord. . . ."*

At the conclusion of the service, the coffin was taken into the side chapel that served as the mortuary of the Russells. Here, amid monuments of the family's dynastic glory—facsimiles, in marble and alabaster, of stars, garters, and coronets—the remains of the dead man were laid to rest.

The next day, Courvoisier was committed by the magistrates for trial and taken to Newgate.

CHAPTER SEVEN

Witness for the Prosecution

sit thou a patient looker-on:
Judge not the play before the play is done.

—Quarles

On Thursday, June 18, 1840, the Old Bailey was from an early hour crowded with illustrious personages—peers of the realm, foreign diplomatists, a royal duke. The air was sultry, and ladies of rank and fashion vainly sought to counteract the effects of the heat through a liberal use of fans and bouquets.

At ten o'clock, Courvoisier, looking "very pale, but perfectly composed," was brought into the court and placed in the dock. The Clerk of the Arraigns read the indictment and afterwards apprised the prisoner that, as a foreigner, he had the privilege of being tried by a jury composed of both foreigners and Englishmen. Courvoisier waived the privilege and said that he was content to be tried by Englishmen.

The jury was sworn, and the judges came in. Lord Chief Justice Tindal, who had presided at the trial of Greenacre, and Mr. Baron Parke,* a judge of the Exchequer of Pleas, took their places on the bench. When the prisoner was asked how he pled, he responded, in a feeble voice, "Not guilty." Mr. Adolphus then rose to open the case for the prosecution. The powers of the great advocate, who was now in his seventy-second year, were manifestly declining. For want of better arguments, he was reduced to playing upon the Englishman's congenital distrust of foreigners, who, he said, did not like to rob a man unless they murdered him first, "for they imagined that if they destroyed the life of the person they robbed, there would exist no testimony against them." But such forensic slumming could not make up for the weaknesses in the Crown's case, and Mr. Adolphus was unable to account either for the missing silver or the absence of bloody linen. It is true, as we have seen, that two dirty handkerchiefs with "spots or marks of blood on them" were found in Courvoisier's portmanteau; and after he was taken into custody, a pair of white cotton gloves, lightly stained with blood, was discovered in the same place.** But in a masterly cross-examination, the defense counsel, the Anglo-Irish lawyer Charles Phillips,*** broke down Constable Baldwin's claim that he was not aware that as a result of such discoveries (which were made only after the initial police searches had taken place), he and his fellow officers were eligible for reward money. When, after Phillips finished tossing and goring the hapless Baldwin, the court adjourned for the day, knowledgeable observers were of the opinion that the

---

* Born at Highfield, near Liverpool, in 1782; Trinity College, Cambridge; called to the Bar by the Inner Temple in 1813; raised to the King's Bench in 1828; a Baron of the Exchequer from 1833.

** In charging the jury, Lord Chief Justice Tindal told the jurors that they "must give no credit" whatever to Constable Baldwin's statements concerning the bloodstained handkerchiefs and gloves.

*** Born at Sligo circa 1787; Trinity College, Dublin; called to the Irish Bar in 1812, to the English, in 1821.

Crown's case was in jeopardy of miscarrying; and in the clubs, "the betting was heavily in favour of Courvoisier's acquittal."

———•———

When, the next day, the court met again, there occurred one of those reversals of fortune which savor more of the theatricality of the stage than the mundaneness of real life. Rumors that a significant discovery had been made were already abroad when the prisoner took his place in the dock. The reporter for *The Times* thought "he appeared more anxious and depressed than on the previous day," and the sergeant-at-law told him that he might be accommodated with a chair. The offer, however, was declined.

A little before ten, the judges came in and took their seats on the bench. The suspense was great as Mr. Adolphus rose to tell the court that on the previous afternoon, a most important piece of information had come to the attention of the prosecution. Mr. Phillips rose instantly to protest. "In justice to the prisoner," he said, "a communication of the facts should have been made to me as soon as they came to the knowledge of the prosecution."

"I believe the communication took place as soon as possible," Adolphus replied.

Phillips continued to remonstrate, but the Lord Chief Justice silenced him. "Let us have no more inquiry or argument about it. Call the next witness."

The suspense, however, continued, for only after the prosecution witnesses previously scheduled to testify were called would the new and mysterious witness for the Crown appear.

At last the moment came.

"Call Charlotte Piolaine," said the clerk of the court.

A woman dressed in black entered the room. Courvoisier had, until that moment, preserved "the greatest composure," Adolphus wrote in his diary; but upon seeing the witness, "he became most agitated, gushed into a profuse perspiration and nearly fainted."

The witness was sworn and, examined by Adolphus, gave her name as Charlotte Piolaine. "My husband's name is Louis—he is a Frenchman—I am an Englishwoman—we keep the Hotel Dieppe, Leicester Place, Leicester Square." The witness was asked whether she knew the prisoner in the dock. She did. "I think it is about four years ago that I knew him—he came to a situation, to take a place in the hotel as waiter—I do not recollect whether he told me his name—we used to call him *Jean*—French is generally spoken at our hotel. . . ."

"Since that time, has the prisoner continued to be acquainted with you, coming in occasionally?"

"I never saw him since till about six weeks ago I think—he then came to our hotel—it was on a Sunday evening—he merely asked me how I was—he stayed about two minutes."

"How did he introduce himself to you, do you remember?"

"He knocked at the room door, I said, 'Come in,' and he walked in—I did not recognize who he was at the moment—it was some time since I had seen him—he said, 'Do not you recollect me?'—I said, 'No, I do not'—he said, 'I am John, that used to live with you some time, over in the Square'—I recollected him then—he stayed a few minutes, and then went away. . . . I saw him again, I think it was on . . . a Sunday evening—he merely came in and asked me how I was—it was in the evening—he had a paper parcel in his hand—he asked me if I would take care of it till the Tuesday following, and he would call for it—I said, certainly I would, and he left it with me, and went away—I put the parcel in a closet, and locked it up—it is a closet I use generally—I had no notion at that time what the parcel contained—it was a sort of round parcel, tied with a string, and sealed."

"Did he call for it on the Tuesday following?"

"I never saw him since until to-day. . . . I took the parcel out of the closet yesterday morning, for the first time—I was induced to take it out, on account of what my cousin brought upstairs in a French newspaper—he read it to me, and showed it to me."

Mme. Piolaine testified that the parcel, when she opened it, contained, together with such things as stockings and an old coat, a number of silver spoons and forks. Each of the utensils was stamped with a crest distinguished by a goat *statant* (standing in profile with its four feet upon the ground).

It was the crest of the Russells.

In cross-examining Mme. Piolaine, Phillips attempted to discredit her testimony by insinuating that the Hotel Dieppe was a house of ill repute, but to no avail, and a succession of prosecution witnesses corroborated her story. A washerwoman testified that the stockings found in the parcel belonged to Courvoisier, while his great friend Carr told the court that the coat, too, was his. A print-seller in Pall Mall testified that the brown paper in which the parcel was enveloped was the same he had used to wrap *The Vision of Ezekiel*, a print which Lord William had recently acquired from him; and the identity of the silver was proved by his lordship's former valet, James Ellis, who was now valet to Lord Mansfield, a relative of the great eighteenth-century jurist William Murray, first Earl of Mansfield.

When, a short time later, the court adjourned for the day, Courvoisier sent a message to his counsel: "Tell Mr. Phillips, my counsel, that I consider my life is in his hands."

CHAPTER EIGHT

A Bad Brief

I walked, with other souls in pain,
Within another ring,
And was wondering if the man had done
A great or little thing,
When a voice behind me whispered low,
"That fellow's got to swing."

—Oscar Wilde

Had the appearance of Charlotte Piolaine as a witness for the prosecution been Charles Phillips's only surprise that day, he might have considered himself fortunate. But Phillips's difficulties were compounded by a circumstance known, at the time, only to a few of those who watched him in his last, desperate struggle to save his client's life. Earlier in the morning, as Phillips sat in the courtroom awaiting the judges, Courvoisier had turned to him and said that he had something to tell him in confidence.

What had happened was this. Courvoisier had been taking exercise that morning in the press yard with the other prisoners. Unbeknownst to him, the police had taken Mme. Piolaine to a room overlooking the press yard, where she had at once identified him as the man she knew as "Jean." The police then informed Courvoisier that a witness had come forward with the missing plate and had identified him as the man who had brought it to her.

In his conference with Phillips, Courvoisier admitted that it was true—that he *had* given the parcel with the plate to Mme. Piolaine.

Phillips, who until that moment had been persuaded of his client's innocence, was speechless. At last he said, "Of course then you are going to plead guilty?"

"No, sir," Courvoisier replied. "I expect you to defend me to the uttermost."

Phillips was inclined to throw up his brief; but after consulting one of the judges, Mr. Baron Parke, he conceived that, as his client would not release him from his obligation, he had no choice but to carry on. The brief was indeed a bad one—could scarcely have been worse; but Phillips rose to the occasion, so much so that he was afterwards criticized—quite unfairly—for having defended too zealously a man whom he knew to be guilty. But the zeal was in vain; no amount of forensic ingenuity could have overcome the testimony of Mme. Piolaine.

The next morning, Saturday, June 20, 1840, the court met again, and Phillips made his closing address to the jury. It was, an old lawyer who heard it remembered, "extremely eloquent." But the brilliant advocate was "overweighted by facts," and English juries are not "apt to be carried away by flowers of rhetoric."

————•————

The solution to the mystery of the purloined plate spelled the doom of Courvoisier; and after deliberating for an hour and a half, the jurors returned a verdict of guilty. Lord Chief Justice Tindal assumed the black cap and pronounced the sentence of death.

In retrospect, the crime and punishment of Courvoisier marked the end of an era. The hideousness of the crime was overshadowed by the absorbing puzzle of its solution. This was less because of Lord William's unsympathetic character as a victim—he seemed to some a senescent parasite—than on account of the change in literary and cultural modes that was taking place. The Romantic rebels who had risen up to shatter the neo-classical idols of their eighteenth-century fathers were themselves in decline. They had rejected the detached, ironical empiricism of the Enlightenment and had revived, in its place, the bloody poetries of the past. Yet now their own candles were guttering down. Scott was in his grave. So were Lamb, Shelley, Keats, Byron, and Coleridge. Wordsworth was, indeed, alive, but his genius, it is generally conceded, was no longer so.[*] In murder-writing as in the other departments of literature, a new empiricism, a brusque, commonsensical style of writing and perception, was coming into favor, one reflective of a larger alteration in the culture as a whole. The new style, if it conveyed accurately enough the surface perplexities of particular crimes, was incapable of penetrating their depths.

It is true that in May 1840 two Romantic prose-masters were living who might have found in the Mayfair murder something more than a test of deductive wit, a cryptogram in flesh and blood. Had these writers interested themselves in the case, they might have left a more probing account of it than is found in the

---

[*] The correlative Romanticism in religion was similarly in decline. The Oxford Movement effectively ended with the cessation of the *Tracts for the Times* following the appearance of Newman's Tract 90 in 1841: four years later, Newman was received into the Roman Catholic Church. The Romantic Toryism of Young England survived, if it did not flourish, in the 1840s, and was given its finest literary expression in three novels Disraeli published in that decade: *Coningsby* (1844), *Sybil* (1845), and *Tancred* (1847). But in his ascent to the top of the greasy pole, Disraeli discarded his youthful philosophy; the charms of romance paled before the more potent pleasures of power.

surviving sources. At the very least they would have been sensitive to the subtler reverberations of its atmosphere; would have seen the ghosts at the windows, sniffed the rotting feudalisms in the cellar—perceived the molding of new crimes out of old ones. The house of Russell boasted a castle ascendancy as gruesome as those of Borgia and Atreus; and in other circumstances Thomas Carlyle might have delighted to expose it. But it so fell out that on the afternoon of Tuesday, May 5, 1840—Lord William's last—he was delivering the first of six lectures on heroes and hero-worship in Portman Square. Carlyle thought lecturing akin to being murdered, an "absolute martyrdom," but he had to go through with it, and during the whole of May his powers were narrowly focused on Portman Square.

As for De Quincey, he was now fifty-five, a widower and functioning *opiomane* living with his children in a cottage on the outer fringe of Edinburgh. His mind was as fertile as ever, and his pen as productive; but in the spring of 1840 he was seeing the final installments of his *Recollections of the Lake Poets* through the press, and like Carlyle he had little time to spare. He seems also to have looked on Courvoisier's murder-artistry as unfinished, and in his 1854 essay, "Three Memorable Murders," he referred, on I am not sure what evidence, to "the scheme of Courvoisier" to "have sought each separate month's support in a separate well-concerted murder," a scheme which, if it had been projected, was never realized.

CHAPTER NINE

Shrift

He turned over the leaves. Carelessly at first; but,
lighting on a passage which attracted his attention,
he soon became intent upon the volume. It was a
history of the lives and trials of great criminals;
and the pages were soiled and thumbed with use.
Here he read of dreadful crimes that made the
blood run cold; of secret murders that had been
committed by the lonely wayside; of bodies hidden
from the eye of man in deep pits and wells: which
would not keep them down, deep as they were, but
had yielded them up at last, after many years, and
so maddened the murderers with the sight, that
in their horror they had confessed their guilt, and
yelled for the gibbet to end their agony.

—*Dickens, Oliver Twist*

Courvoisier, returned to Newgate a condemned man, fell
into a depression of spirits. He was "sullen and reserved,"
and he tried, unsuccessfully, to end his life by stuffing a

towel down his throat. By degrees, however, he recovered something of his old equanimity; he made friends with his jailers, who came to feel a genuine affection for him; he prayed to God; and he composed a number of confessions in which he did not scruple to admit that he was, indeed, the killer of Lord William.

There were at least five of these exercises in shrift. In the first, he said that the murder was the result of a quarrel. Late Tuesday night (as he told it), Lord William rang the bell. Thinking that his lordship wanted his bed warmed, he went upstairs with the warming pan. His lordship was not pleased with this anticipation of his desires; he said that a valet ought not to presume to know his master's wishes, and "ought always to go and answer the bell first, to see what [was] wanted." A little after midnight, Lord William rang again; this time, he said, he *did* want his bed warmed, and added, "rather crossly," that Courvoisier should take "more notice of what he was doing." By now Courvoisier was himself very angry, and in a fit of pique, he says, went downstairs and set about disarranging the dining room. Lord William, when he came down to use the water closet, caught him in the act. "What are you doing here?" he asked. "You have no good intentions in doing this; you must quit my service tomorrow morning; and I shall acquaint your friends with it." He then went up to his bedroom, leaving Courvoisier in great agitation. He concluded that the "only way" he could cover his "faults" was by murdering his master:

> This was the first moment any idea of the sort entered into my head. I went into the dining room and took a knife from the side-board. I do not remember whether it was a carving knife or not. I then went up stairs. I opened his bedroom door and heard him snoring in his sleep; there was a rushlight in his room burning at this time. I went near the bed by the side of the window, and then I murdered him; he just moved his arm a little; he never spoke a word. I took a towel which was on the back

of the chair, and wiped my hand and the knife . . . the
towel I put over his face. . . .

This confession provoked much skepticism. Would Lord William really have taken no precautions for his safety after having discovered a man whom he had only recently taken into his service in the act of pillaging his house? Would he really have returned to his bedroom and gone peaceably to sleep after he had not only fired the man, but rendered him desperate by saying that he would acquaint others with his conduct?

Courvoisier himself seems to have recognized that the confession was not credible, and he soon offered another version of events. He now blamed the murder, not on a quarrel with his master which culminated in violence, but on the deleterious effects of strong drink on a young man unused to wine; the intoxicating fumes, he said, betrayed him into madness. Yet since his imprisonment a great change had come over him: he had rediscovered God and been regenerated in Christ. The confession culminates in his edifying realization that Jesus "is his friend." The skeptical reader, however, may perhaps be forgiven for wondering whether Courvoisier's account of his redemption was not calculated to appeal to the sympathies of a pious and Evangelical age, and contrived with the ulterior motive of obtaining the commutation of an appalling sentence.

———•———

As the day of his death drew nearer and hopes of a reprieve grew fainter, Courvoisier made another, more believable confession, in which he traced the history of his life from boyhood and described how, as he grew to man's estate, his moral and religious scruples gradually fell away. On his entry into Lord William's service, he says, his morals, though far from perfect, were still comparatively pure; he would have shuddered at the thought of committing a really base or bloody act. The occasion of his downfall, he says, was the journey during which he attended Lord William to Richmond. In that fashionable gathering place he found himself much in the company of other servants, many of whom had seen a good deal more of the world than he had. Their talk of the beauty of "different scenes (towns, villages, country houses)" opened for him a new and enchanting prospect; and seduced by wanderlust, he resolved to exchange his tedious employment in Norfolk Street for the agreeable indolence of the aimless traveler.

But travel costs money, and Courvoisier was short of funds. And so he began, in his words, "to premeditate the seizure" of Lord William's gold and banknotes. He knew, of course, that if he stooped to robbery, he would be professedly a villain; but he had been reading a "history of thieves and murderers" which convinced him that crime was not only an amusing but, in its own way, an honorable occupation. "I read the book with pleasure," he said, and by a dexterous casuistry he persuaded himself that it would not "be a great sin to place" himself among the lawbreakers. "On the contrary," he said, "I admired their skill and their valour. I was particularly struck with the history of a young man who was born of very respectable parents, and who had spent his property in gaming and debauchery, and afterwards went from place to place stealing all he could. I admired his cunning, instead of feeling horrified at it. . . ."[*]

At first, he said, he intended only to rob Lord William. But he afterwards determined that, if he were to cover his traces, he must kill him. The robbery would thereby "be better concealed," and "I should have done with him all at once, and be ready for my journey." The decision taken, he made up the package of pilfered

---

[*] It is often said that the book in question was the Newgate novel *Jack Sheppard* by W. Harrison Ainsworth; but it was more likely one of the innumerable *Newgate Calendars* then in circulation, books which are to heroic crime what Plutarch's *Lives* are to heroic statesmanship and make the same, simultaneous appeal both to some of the basest and some of the loftiest human passions.

plate and carried it one evening to the Hotel Dieppe, where he confided it into the hands of Mme. Piolaine. The next step, however, was infinitely harder, and Courvoisier hesitated to take it. He had, he said, "an evil thought of putting my hand to the work" on Monday, the fourth of May, but a "remnant of conscience" restrained him. The next day was Tuesday, the fifth. He and Lord William "had some altercation" over the unsent carriage, but the quarrel, he said, was a trifling one, "not worth the while to speak of." Nevertheless, he was resolved: Lord William must die. After warming his master's bed that night, he went downstairs, and when all was quiet he opened various drawers and cupboards to make it look as though the house had been ransacked. (Novices who contrive to make it appear as though a robbery has taken place are apt to exaggerate the element of anarchic wildness in such crimes; the experienced housebreaker is, as a rule, precise and methodical.)

Courvoisier then fetched a knife in the dining room and mounted the staircase to Lord William's bedroom. "When I opened the door I heard him asleep, and stopped for a while, thinking of what I was about to do; but the evil disposition of my heart did not allow me to repent. I turned up my coat and shirtsleeve, and came near to the bed on the side of the window. There I heard a cry of my conscience, telling me, 'Thou art doing wrong'; but I hardened myself against this voice, and threw myself on my victim, and murdered him with the knife I was holding in my right hand. I wiped my hand and the knife with a towel, which I placed on the face of Lord William."

CHAPTER TEN

"There It Stands, Black and Ready"

Now was there ever any man seen to sleep in the cart,
between Newgate, and Tyburn? between the prison,
and the place of execution, does any man sleep?

—*John Donne*

Courvoisier's newly awakened Christian piety did not prevent him, as the day of his doom approached, from longing for a pagan death. With considerable cunning he managed to secrete, in the depths of the mattress in his cell, a piece of wood sharp enough to open a vein. But the intuition of Mr. Cope, the governor of Newgate, frustrated his desire for the dignity of a Roman end. On the eve of the execution, Cope ordered a search of Courvoisier's cell and person to be made; and he could afterwards flatter himself that, as a result of this charitable vigilance, the condemned man, though he would suffer the last agony of the scaffold, would be mercifully spared a self-induced death which might have exposed his soul to a hotter hellfire.

The fatal day came—Monday, July 6, 1840. Courvoisier rose at four o'clock that morning and busied himself in writing letters. Around seven, the Swiss Minister in London came in, followed by a party of noblemen and members of Parliament eager to observe the behavior of a man who is about to be hanged. At half past seven, Courvoisier received Holy Communion, and he afterwards gave away, to those who had shown him kindness in prison, his little collection of books. "O God!" he cried at one point, "how could I have committed so dreadful a crime? It was madness! When I think of it I cannot believe it."

Calcraft, the executioner, made his appearance. From a black bag he drew a piece of rope, and with it he pinioned the arms and wrists of the prisoner. The prison chaplain, the Rev. Mr. Carver, asked Courvoisier "whether he was fully penitent for the crime he had committed, and whether he believed in the atonement of the Saviour." Courvoisier replied, in "barely audible whispers," that he was and did. Yet his face, it is said, showed "but too plainly" the "deep anguish of his soul."

———◆———

Outside Newgate, the customary carnival atmosphere prevailed. Yet there were those in the crowd who were far from sharing in the general jubilation. Among these was William Makepeace Thackeray, who at the time was writing for *Fraser's Magazine* and contributing book reviews to *The Times*; the novels with which he was to make his reputation were yet to be written. The sight of the gallows struck him, he said, with the force of an electric shock. "There it stands," he wrote, "black and ready, jutting out from a little door in the prison."

His qualms bore witness to the great revulsion in public feeling that was then taking place. During the previous decade, the number of executions in England had fallen off sharply, and juries were now reluctant to send their fellow creatures to the gallows for any crime short of murder. In 1829, twenty-four people had been hanged in London for crimes *other* than murder; but between 1832 and 1844 not a single person was hanged *except* for murder. Yet the rarer the public hangings grew, the more intense the disgust they excited in those who opposed them. When, in the eighteenth century, the "Bloody Code" was in effect, scarcely anyone batted an eye as whole cartloads of human beings, male and female, were taken to Tyburn to suffer the last penalty of the law. Respectable opinion, indeed, held that such spectacles had a salutary influence on the lower orders. The seventeenth-century landowner and traveler Sir Henry Blount "was wont to say that he did not care to have his servants goe to church, for there servants infected one another to goe to the alehouse and learn debauchery; but he did bid them goe to see the executions at Tyburne, which worke more upon them than all the oratory in the sermons." But times had changed, and the outrage expressed by Thackeray was to culminate, a quarter of a century later, in the abolition of public hangings in Britain.*

———•———

Courvoisier had, in his latest confession, disburdened himself of all but the very last mystery that shrouded his crime—a secret he might have taken with him to the grave had not Evans, one of the under-sheriffs, put the question to him that morning. How, Evans asked, was it "possible he could cut the throat of his unfortunate master without leaving a trace of blood" on his clothes? When, previously, Courvoisier had been asked this question, he had replied

---

* The Capital Punishment Amendment Act of 1868, which received royal assent on May 29, 1868, ended public executions in the United Kingdom. Hangings thereafter took place within the walls of the prison in which the condemned man or woman was then incarcerated. Michael Barrett was the last person publicly hanged in the kingdom: convicted of bombing Coldbath Fields Prison in an attempt to liberate Fenian prisoners, he died on the gallows at Newgate on May 26, 1868.

that he had turned up the sleeves of his coat and his shirt. Now, having reached the sea mark of his life's utmost sail, he told the truth. "His answer," Evans said, "was that he had no clothes on: he committed the crime in a complete state of nudity, and he only had to wash himself at the sink on coming down."*

———•———

The bell of St. Sepulchre began to toll the knell. An "immense sway and movement," Thackeray said, "swept over the whole of that vast, dense crowd." The men instantly "uncovered"—took off their hats—and "a great murmur arose, more awful, *bizarre*, and indescribable than any sound I had ever heard before."

Courvoisier appeared, and mounted the steps to the gallows; Calcraft followed. It was just after eight o'clock.

In the opinion of most of the observers who afterwards recorded, in the formulaic phrases of the time, their impressions of the event, Courvoisier acquitted himself well. He displayed, it was said, an extraordinary nerve. His step "was steady and collected," and his countenance, though pale, was "calm and unmoved." Thackeray, with his artist's second sight, saw a very different man, one who "turned his head here and there" and "looked about him for an instant with a wild, imploring look."

The noose was placed around Courvoisier's neck and the hood drawn over his head. He clasped his hands one within the other and lifted up his head, perhaps in supplication. The bolt was withdrawn, and he died without a struggle; he was twenty-three. After hanging for an hour, the body was cut down and taken into Newgate, where it was buried, that evening, in Birdcage Walk.

---

* It is possible that Courvoisier emulated one of the heroes of the *Newgate Calendar*, James Hall, a servant who in June 1741 murdered his master, John Penny, in his chambers in Clement's Inn. To avoid getting blood on his clothes, Hall stripped himself naked before he cut his master's throat.

PART FOUR

Toward the Ripper

The finest trick of the devil is to persuade you
that he does not exist.

—*Baudelaire*

CHAPTER ONE

Wapping

Nor can I refuse myself to those events, which,
from their uncommon magnitude, will interest a
philosophic mind in the history of blood.

—Gibbon

D e Quincey was apt to be picky about his murderers. In his
1827 satire, "On Murder Considered as One of the Fine
Arts," he makes his imaginary lecturer, addressing the
Society of Connoisseurs in Murder, conclude that Jack Thurtell's
murder of Weare was "much overrated." There was "something
falsetto" in the man's style which forbade his induction into the
pantheon of really remarkable killers. De Quincey always held that
the *ne plus ultra* of homicidal horrors were those that took place in
the purlieus of Wapping in December 1811, killings so gruesome, he
wrote in "Three Memorable Murders," that in committing them the
transgressor asserted his "supremacy above all the children of Cain."

Undoubtedly, what De Quincey called the "scenical features" of the murders contributed to the impression of horror they left upon the mind. The very name, *Wapping*, savors of something disgusting. The district lay in the "most chaotic quarter of eastern or nautical London," where, De Quincey said, a "manifold ruffianism" was "shrouded impenetrably under the mixed hats and turbans of men whose past was untraceable to any European eye." He shuddered to contemplate the sinister "Lascars, Chinese, Moors, and Negroes" who were to be met at every step, yet he conceded that the delinquencies of seafaring Asians and Africans were no more terrible than those of their European counterparts, the navies of Christendom being, in his estimation, "the sure receptacle" of all those "murderers and ruffians" whose crimes gave them a "motive for withdrawing themselves for a season from the public eye."

Wapping's ambiguous and even sinister reputation was not new. During several centuries, pirates were hanged there, on a gibbet near the low-water mark of the Thames. In the eighteenth century, a network of tenements overspread the marshy lowlands, where the air was heavy with the odors of cesspools and tidal sludge; in the rancid streets, cheap lodging houses stood cheek by jowl with ale-houses and gin-shops that catered to sailors on the spree. De Quincey's own knowledge of the district perhaps owed something to another of its characteristic features, the innumerable dens where, at any hour of the day or night, an assortment of spectral figures, ravaged by opium, might be found in supine thrall to the juice of the poppy.

Hard times compounded the misery of Wapping in 1811. As a result of Napoleon's Continental Blockade, trade between Britain and Europe had fallen off precipitously, with British exports declining by as much as one half. It was the winter of Luddism and scarce food; and in Wapping ship-chandlers, sail-makers, and anchor-smiths, whose livelihoods depended on the sea, struggled to make ends meet, while out-of-work sailors, released from shipboard constraints, fell into a kind of feral life.

CHAPTER TWO

The Murder of the Marrs

All other murders look pale by the deep crimson
of his ...
—De Quincey

The night, De Quincey said, was one of exceeding darkness. A little before midnight, a young merchant named
Timothy Marr was preparing to close his silk-and-linen
shop in the Ratcliffe Highway, on the northern edge of Wapping.
With him, in the dwelling that served him both as a workplace and
a residence, was his young wife, Celia; their three-month-old son,
Timothy Junior; a Devonshire lad, James Gowen, whom Marr had
engaged as an apprentice; and Margaret Jewell, a young woman
who was the family's maid-of-all-work.

Marr was twenty-four years old on this particular Saturday,
December 7, 1811. Before taking up silk mercery and linen draping,
he had been a sailor aboard the *Dover Castle*, an East Indiaman.

His new mode of getting a living, if it was more settled than his previous one, was no less laborious, and long after darkness had fallen he might be seen, through the window of his shop, hard at work over his merchandise.

On this particular night, Marr was hungry. He gave the girl Margaret Jewell a pound note and told her to fetch some oysters; with the change she was to pay the baker. It was not quite midnight when she set out; she would later remember how, as she left the shop, she saw, on the opposite side of the street, a man's figure in the light of the oil lamp, "stationary at the instant, but in the next instant slowly moving." She withdrew her gaze and went off over the wet cobblestones toward Taylor's oyster shop.

Midnight struck. The night watchman, Mr. Olney, cried the hour as he passed by Marr's house. He afterwards remembered seeing Marr engaged in putting up his shutters. A quarter of an hour later, when he passed the house again, he went (as was his custom) to examine the shutters, to make sure they were fast. They were not. He called to Marr to inform him of the fact.

"We know of it," a voice returned.

In the meantime, Margaret Jewell reached the oyster shop and found it shut. The baker, too, had closed his door for the night. The girl expended some additional minutes in a fruitless search for oysters before making her way back through the silent streets to Marr's house. When she reached it, it was dark. She rang the bell and knocked gently on the door. "She had no fear of disturbing her master or mistress," De Quincey said; her anxiety was rather "for the baby, who, being disturbed, might again rob her mistress of a night's rest." Yet to her consternation, there was neither stir nor murmur within, but rather an unaccountable silence. Margaret Jewell became afraid and "rang the bell with the violence that belongs to sickening terror."

At last there came an answering sound—the creak of a stair. Not, De Quincey says, one of the stairs "that led downwards to the kitchen," but one "that led upwards to the single storey of bedchambers above." Someone was coming down this stair-case: "one, two, three, four, five stairs were slowly and distinctly descended." The sound of footsteps approached the door and ceased. In her terror, Margaret Jewell began "to ring the bell and to ply the knocker with unintermitting violence."

It was near one o'clock now, and Mr. Olney, coming along the highway to cry the hour, perceived Miss Jewell's distress. He went to her and began himself to ring and knock.

"Mr. Marr! Mr. Marr!"

Next door to Marr there lived a pawnbroker called Murray. Exasperated by the noise at his neighbor's door, he rose in something like anger to investigate. But on learning the reason for the disturbance, he became grave. He recalled how, about midnight, he and his family had heard, through the party wall, the sound of a heavy thud, followed by a sort of cry. They had dismissed it as being of no consequence; yet it now wore a different aspect, and Murray went over the garden wall and approached the back of his neighbor's house to see what might be learned. Through the open doorway he perceived a glimmer of candlelight.

He went inside and mounted the staircase. The candle stood on the landing. "Marr, Marr," he said softly, "your window shutters are not fastened." But response there was none. He took the candle and went down to the shop room. Stepping over the threshold, he came across something on the floor. To his horror, he beheld a crumpled figure, a bloody face, a spatter of brains, all lurid in the candlelight. It was young James Gowen, or what remained of him. Turning away, he came upon another corpse: Celia Marr lay face down in a pool of blood. Her throat had been cut, and the left side of her skull was horribly broken. Appalled by the carnage, Murray made his way through a slaughter-house "so floated with gore," De Quincey writes, "that it was hardly possible to escape the pollution of blood in picking out a path to the front door."

He unlocked it to admit Mr. Olney, who came into the house followed by another watchman and an assortment of gapers to find a scene of uniform calamity. The body of the master of the house was discovered behind his counter: Timothy Marr's nose was broken, and the occipital bone at the base of his skull fractured; his face bore the marks of a tremendous blow to the right eye. Three members of the household were positively dead: but what of the baby—where was little Timothy? Search was made, and the infant was found in the kitchen, in his cradle. His innocence had not escaped the wrath or cruelty of the killer. His throat had been cut and his tiny face beaten to a pulp.

CHAPTER THREE

Bloody Revels

my wit's diseased

—*Shakespeare*

I t would be impossible, De Quincey said, to describe "the frenzy of feelings" which news of the Wapping murders excited throughout Britain. For "twelve succeeding days, under some groundless notion that the unknown murderer had quitted London, the panic which had convulsed the mighty metropolis diffused itself all over the island. I was myself at that time nearly three hundred miles from London; but there, and everywhere, the panic was indescribable."

The delirium had not yet subsided when, on the twelfth night following the murders, John Williamson was sitting beside the fire in the King's Arms on New Gravel Lane in Wapping. Fifty-six years old on that mild night, December 19, 1811, Williamson had been the proprietor of the King's Arms since the 1790s. Shortly before eleven o'clock, one of his neighbors, Mr. Anderson, a constable of the parish, came in for a pot of ale.

"You are an officer," Williamson said to Anderson. "There has been a fellow loitering at my door with a brown coat on: if you should see him, take him into custody, or tell me."

"I certainly will," said Constable Anderson, "for my own safety as well as yours." He bade his neighbor good night and went away with his ale.

———•———

The King's Arms was a respectable house, and Mr. Williamson a respectable publican. He had been long enough about his business to know that very little good occurs in a pouring establishment after midnight, and as early as eleven o'clock he began to put up his shutters. On this particular night, four others remained in the house with him: his wife, Elizabeth; his granddaughter, Kitty Stillwell; a middle-aged serving woman, Bridget Harrington; and a lodger, John Turner, a sawyer by trade.

About half past eleven, Constable Anderson, having consumed the last of his ale, left his house to procure some more. He had scarcely come into the street when he was astonished to see a man, practically naked, lowering himself by knotted sheets from an upper window of the King's Arms. The twisted bed linen, however, reached only so far, and upon reaching the end of it the man found himself dangling a dozen or so feet above the New Gravel Road. A passing watchman, perceiving his plight, had gone to his assistance. The naked man dropped into his arms. He was John Turner, Mr. Williamson's lodger, and his face was "as white as a corpse's." "There's murder inside," he said; "he's at it now, killing 'em all."

A crowd had by this time gathered, and Turner's "dreadful annunciation" was received as the signal for action. The bystanders, driven, De Quincey says, by a "passionate enthusiasm," rose as one man to catch "the wolfish dog in the high noon and carnival of his bloody revels—in the very centre of his own shambles."

The door of the King's Arms and the cellar flap were instantly forced, and the crowd rushed in. Mr. Williamson lay in a pool of spreading blood in the basement, beside the stairs that led to the tap room. His head had been beaten bloody; his throat had been cut; and part of his hand had been hacked away. The body of his wife was found in the kitchen; her throat, too, had been cut, and her skull broken. Not far from her lay Bridget Harrington. Her labors were complete: her throat had been cut to the bone. Only the grandchild, the young Kitty Stillwell, was yet living—she had slept through the horror.

CHAPTER FOUR

Subjective Correlative

The phantasms themselves do not believe, or at least affect disbelief, in their own reality, and laughingly style themselves delirium, or hallucination.
—*D. S. Merezhkovsky*

De Quincey was far from being a scrupulous historian of murder. His carelessness in the relation of facts drew upon him the rebuke of William Roughead, who said that he resembled the character in Scott's *The Antiquary*, Sir Arthur Wardour, who disdained a "pettifogging intimacy with dates, names, and trifling matters of fact," a "tiresome and frivolous accuracy of memory. . . ."

Yet much as one may deplore De Quincey's infidelities to fact, his account of the Wapping murders remains the most insightful thing ever to have been written about them. To be sure, he lazily accepted the official version of the case, which held that the murders had been committed by one John Williams, a twenty-seven-year-old sailor. In their meticulous study, *The Maul and the Pear Tree*, P. D. James and T. A. Critchley conclude that Williams was almost certainly *not* the killer, though he may have been one of the killer's accomplices. They finger instead a sailor from Danzig, William Ablass, "Long Billy," who, however, was never brought to trial. Nor indeed did Williams himself have his day in court: not long after his arrest, he was found dead in his cell in Coldbath Fields Prison, "suspended by the neck from an iron bar which crossed the cell."

It is unlikely that the identity of the killer will ever be known with certainty, but whoever he was, De Quincey saw more deeply into the nature of *his* character than any of his contemporaries. Nor, but for De Quincey's guidance, could we who study the case today comprehend just why these particular murders should have been felt, at the time, to be so uniquely and preternaturally appalling. For the Wapping murders do not affect us in the way they did De Quincey and his contemporaries. Not only are they remote from us in time, they have no master-image of grotesquerie capable of closing up the temporal gap, no talisman in which the macabre essence of the thing is efficiently concentrated—no gory head fished up from the depths of a London canal, no loin of pork feasted upon by one who had just beaten a man's brains out in an adjacent lane.

The Wapping murders are no less at a disadvantage in their *mise-en-scène*. Try as I might to worm my way into the evil spirit of that time and place, I am not so immediately, viscerally appalled by the atmosphere as I am, say, by that of such a killing as Julia Wallace's, in the hag-ridden darkness of Depression-era Liverpool, with its attendant circumstances of rain-slick streets, of grime and petrol exhaust, of a solitary telephone booth and a mysterious caller, "R. M. Qualtrough," of 25 Menlove Gardens East. In the Wallace murder, as in those committed by Christie in 10 Rillington Place, I find a quality of horror very nearly related to that which I have been prepared to feel by books like Graham Greene's *The Confidential Agent* and George Orwell's *The Road to*

Wigan Pier, with their aroma of slop pails, greasy cookery, and coal fires burning in sordid lodgings. The bleakness of the Wallace and Christie murders is deepened for me by the police photographs of the crime scenes, which distill their peculiar nausea more effectually than any prose writer can. The image of the soiled water closet in the Wallaces' house at 29 Wolverton Street, with the single clot of blood upon the lavatory, is as harrowing as anything in the purely literary canon of horror.

Not even De Quincey can rival a mid-twentieth-century crime-scene photographer, painting darkly with light; but sketching merely with words, he gets closer to the heart of the Wapping horrors than his coevals Coleridge and Southey, who were as deeply shocked by them. To be sure, it was hardly a feat of intellect, on De Quincey's part, to see that the horror of the killings was heightened by the want of adequate motive. T. S. Eliot said that *Hamlet* was an artistic failure because Shakespeare found no means of expressing the particular emotional complexion of the hero dramatically, in scenes and incidents: the play lacked what Eliot called an "objective correlative," a "set of objects, a situation, a chain of events" which would be the external "formula" of Hamlet's inward despair. In the Wapping murders, the case is reversed. The outward, objective expression of the killer's state of mind, the external "formula," couldn't be clearer—seven bodies savagely done to death. It is the *subjective* correlative that is lacking: what were the passions that found release, that found fulfillment, in such a blood-letting?

Material gain was perhaps the ostensible motive for the Wapping murders; but it was obvious to De Quincey that no mere desire for money could account for the savagery of the slayings. Nor were the murders in any conventional sense crimes of passion. A spurned and brain-sick lover might indeed have sought to avenge himself on the young and reputedly pretty Celia Marr through a murderous vendetta. Yet the same erotic motive could hardly have induced him to murder, with a no less intense ferocity, Mr. and Mrs. Williamson, a couple past fifty, and their middle-aged serving-woman.

CHAPTER FIVE

The Wolf's Paw

> But are they really superstitions? I see these pref-
> erences rather as denoting a kind of wisdom which
> savage races practised spontaneously and the rejec-
> tion of which, by the modern world, is the real
> madness.
>
> —*Claude Lévi-Strauss*

D e Quincey's insight into the deeper evil of the Wapping
murders began with his perception of their close resemblance to a class of evils found in myth and fairytale—
that is to say, to real evils, but evils described in a language that had
long since come to seem childish and fantastic. The folk culture on
which De Quincey drew was concerned to account for what were
known as "bestial" acts, acts so abhorrent they could be explained
only on the supposition that the perpetrators had been supernaturally transformed into (or taken possession by) beasts.

To a modern reader it soon becomes evident that this folklore of bestialism was concerned primarily with offenses which we today should classify as crimes of sexual deviancy, acts of brutal cruelty with an under-flavor of warped sensuality. Thus David Rose and Hugh Evans were hanged at Guildford, in April 1804, for the "bestial" crime of having cut the face of a young woman, Elizabeth Palmer, after Evans said to her, "Damn you, Miss Palmer, I'll spoil your pretty face for you." The Victorian cleric Sabine Baring-Gould was among the first English scholars to see that the old legends were naïve attempts to understand what was in fact a form of mental illness, a pathology which brought its sufferers not merely to ravish or kill their victims, but to defile them in cruel and grotesque ways.

Baring-Gould belonged to a now virtually extinct race of Anglican clerics, cultivated and eccentric, who under the mild yoke of their pastoral labors found leisure to pursue such curious scholarship as beguiled their fancy.* There was the vicar who composed a book on the flowers in Shakespeare, with a great show of horticultural learning, and another who wrote a voluminous account of the treatment of the naked female in antiquity, in which a good deal of prurient erudition is expended on the art of Zeuxis and Praxiteles, the ring of Gyges, the gymnastic exertions of the Spartan girlhood, and the lascivious manners of the Corinthian *hetairai*. Baring-Gould's own strain of inquisitiveness led him to attempt to thread the labyrinth of another *disciplina arcani*, and in his 1865 *Book of Were-Wolves* he delved into the stories of such sick souls as Jacques Roulet (the "werewolf of Angers") and Jean Grenier (the "French wolf boy"), early serial killers who were

---

* Among his other accomplishments, Rev. Baring-Gould composed the words of the hymn "Onward, Christian Soldiers." He also, unusually for one of his class in that age, engaged himself to marry the daughter of a mill hand from the West Riding of Yorkshire. Grace Taylor was sent to York for two years to acquire genteel manners, and in 1868 the couple were married in Wakefield. The marriage was happy.

thought to have been supernaturally transformed into beasts when they committed their crimes.

What startled Baring-Gould was less the superstitious explanations of the various murders and disappearances than the fact that such explanations should still have been current in the France of the 1860s. He described how, in a provincial village in Poitou-Charentes, the Mayor warned him against crossing a certain stretch of land near Champigny-le-Sec after dark: "Monsieur can never go back tonight across the flats, because of the—the . . . the *loups-garoux* (werewolves)."

A little reflection, however, convinced Baring-Gould that a normal human being might indeed prefer, if only unconsciously, to overlook the brutal facts of certain kinds of crimes, and to draw over them a supernatural veil of lycanthropy, witchcraft, or vampirism. He saw that, as a species, human beings do not like too much reality: when facts make us uncomfortable, we seek refuge in the quasi-truths of myth. Child-murder, torture, cannibalism—the morbidities in question were, Baring-Gould saw, so "ghastly and revolting" that it was only natural that people should have been "disposed to regard as a myth that which the feared investigation might prove a reality."*

De Quincey himself had, of course, no belief in the actual transmogrification of men into beasts: he used the old language of

---

* The case of Andreas Bichel, the Bavarian *Mädchenshclächter* (girl-butcher), was characteristic of those of Baring-Gould's volume. Bichel, he writes, "enticed young women into his house, under the pretence that he was possessed of a magic mirror, in which he would show them their future husbands; when he had them in his power he bound their hands behind their backs, and stunned them with a blow. He then despoiled them of their clothes. . . ." A catalogue of reputed beast-men would include Gilles de Rais, the fifteenth-century child murderer; Peter Stumpp, the sixteenth-century Rhenish killer known as the "Werewolf of Bedburg"; Jacques Rollet, burned at the stake as a *loup-garou* in the Place de Grève in 1577; Thiess of Kaltenbrun; the so-called "werewolfs" of Châlons, Dole, and Auvergne; Martin Dumollard, the "vampire of Lyon"; and Manuel Romasanta, the "werewolf of Allariz" in Spanish Galicia.

bestiality figuratively and imaginatively, to describe evils about which the educated Englishman of his day was considerably more in the dark than the unlettered French peasant. The Englishman was between two worlds: he had lost touch with all that was true in the old myths (to which the peasant still clung), but he had not yet attained the lucidity of modern science. De Quincey sought to enlighten him: he used the archaic language of myth to understand abnormalities which were inexpressible in the conventional language of his day; and he did so with an acuity of insight that anticipated that of the modern scientific investigator.

CHAPTER SIX

Tory Murder

Like most odd and old ideas, it has much truth.

—*Bagehot*

A "bloodhound," a "wolfish dog," a fiend with a "tiger's heart"—so De Quincey paints the Wapping murderer, whom he took to be the sailor Williams. He has it on good authority, he says, that Williams's hair resembled that of a tiger, being "of the most extraordinary and vivid colour,— viz. bright yellow, something between an orange and a lemon colour." The man's hair was an outward sign of his inward "tiger character," as was also his sinister complexion, which "wore at all times a bloodless ghastly pallor."

It is true that this picture of Williams, with his "cadaverous ghastliness," his "extraordinary hair," and his "glazed eyes," has only the slenderest connection to ascertainable fact.* But like the opium-inspired meditations of the *Confessions of an English Opium-Eater*, it is not without its kernel of truth. As much as Richard von Krafft-Ebing, who would identify the pathology of "lust-murder" in his 1886 book *Psychopathia Sexualis*, De Quincey is alive to the erotic element in such crimes. Circumstances, he said, might oblige Williams to hurry his killings, but in "a murder of pure voluptuousness" he would take his time, in order to revel in the "unnatural luxury" of the slaughter, and to satisfy his "wolfish craving for bloodshed." De Quincey used words like "luxury" and "voluptuousness" in their strictly concupiscent sense: he meant to finger the misdirected desires that led the killer to seek his highest sensual gratifications in killing. The killer's "wolfish" instincts are, for De Quincey, a form of debauched Eros, for he seeks not to caress and adore the flesh, but to destroy it.

The Wapping slaughterer was at once a wolf and an aesthete: De Quincey says of the slaughter of the Marrs that it was the *"début"* of an "artist." He compares the killer to a malignant painter, the dark cousin of Titian, Rubens, and van Dyck. Like them, the wolf of Wapping has diverted a portion of his natural passion away from its natural outlet. The artist, according to Plato, has been endowed by the Muses with the supreme creative gift of Eros, but only on condition that he devote the first fruits of its power not to mundane sexual commerce, but to art, to poetic creation. De Quincey's murderous man is a morbid variation of the type, his own fund of erotic power being held in trust not, as it were, for the Muses, but for the devil.

---

* De Quincey drew extensively on the Wapping murders in his 1838 tale *The Avenger*, which describes a mass-murderer whose "human tiger-passion" rages "unchained" in a German city in 1816; but the most original insights of "Three Memorable Murders" are in the story sacrificed to the conventions of nineteenth-century melodrama.

As much as Ibsen, De Quincey knew that the trolls and goblins of myth are real, only, like Ibsen, he saw that they are not (as our ancestors supposed) outside of us, but inside. The old folk languages, however crude they might have been, were for his purposes superior to the ready-made idioms of his own day. The English prose of his time was formed largely on the models of eighteenth-century writers; and the eighteenth-century mind, if it was, as T. S. Eliot said, a mature one, was also, where the deeper springs of human passion are concerned, a shallow one. Compared to De Quincey's portrait of Williams, Gibbon's sketch of Commodus, the depraved tyrant "with an insatiate thirst of human blood," is psychologically naïve: as instruments with which to probe the deeper recesses of mind and feeling, Gibbon's enlightened and neo-classical vocabularies are less supple than De Quincey's archaic-mythical ones.

As both a prose-writer and an historian of murder, De Quincey is a disciple of his hero, Edmund Burke: he uses the resources of the past to understand the complexities of the present. In this he resembles his contemporary Charles Lamb, who pillaged the old authors to form a prose "villainously pranked" with "antique modes and phrases," but only in order that he might convey states of mind wholly modern. In the same way, De Quincey, who is closer in spirit to the unreformed prose masters who wrote before Swift than he is to Gibbon and Dr. Johnson, makes no fetish of the archaic, is always a *modern* ancient; and his antiquated style is the bearer of truths which are even now not obsolete.

De Quincey is the Tory historian of murder; but he wrote in an age of triumphant Whiggism, and was not understood. Nowhere is his insight into the erotically deformed killer more penetrating than when he argues that his malady is not acute but chronic. "All perils, specially malignant," he says, "are recurrent." The man with a taste for "unnatural luxury" does not "relapse into inertia": he continues to seek satisfactions which are, for him, the only "condiment" capable of "seasoning the insipid monotonies of daily life."

De Quincey warned that the sexually sullen man, nursing an erotic grudge against the world, would not be content to strike once: if he got the chance, he would strike again and again. He further believed that there would be more such men in the future. He lamented the "gathering agitation of our present English life," with its "fierce condition of eternal hurry": it was productive of "so chaotic a tumult" that the "eye of the calmest observer" was troubled. Modernity was an acid, one that rapidly corroded customs and restraints that in the past had done something to restrain the sick man's more vicious impulses. At the same time, the monster-cities of the modern world gave such a soul a new habitat in which to hunt: he found a protective coloration in the anonymity of the urban crowd, with which he could blend himself more easily than his counterparts in less congested ages.

De Quincey was a prophet; but like those of Cassandra, his prophecies were not believed. The evil that was not comprehended could not be rooted out; it flourished unnoticed, and like an unpruned weed assumed ever more rankly luxuriant forms. At last, a quarter of a century after De Quincey's death, it assumed a form so malignant that it could no longer be overlooked.

CHAPTER SEVEN

The Autumn Rose

And not far from me is the place where the Tauric
altar of the quivered Goddess is fed with dreadful
slaughter.

—*Ovid*

I t sometimes happens that a cultural form reaches its perfection
only at the end of the generative season, when it blossoms with a
fragrance which, amid so many presages of decay, seems sweeter
than the perfumes of the prime. Such was the philosophy of Plato,
the last expression of the pure original genius of Hellas before its
extinguishment. Such was the antique virtue of Brutus and Cato as
it flowered in a degenerate age of Caesarian dictatorship, the final
vestige of the old republicanism of Rome before it succumbed to the
corruptions of empire. Such, too, was that last and sweetest fruit
of English Gothic art, the chapel of the King's College, Cambridge,
crowned with pinnacles that asserted the pathos of a declining medi-
aevalism in the very dawn of English Renaissance.

The phenomenon of the autumn rose is not unknown in the morphology of murder: but, like all the flowers of evil, it blossoms only blackly. It was the great ambition of the Romantic poets to isolate a strain of horror that would rival those of Moloch-Dionysus antiquity, lust flowering hard by hate in "wanton rites . . . besmeared with blood." But the springtide of Romanticism yielded only inferior blossoms: Byron's incests, Coleridge's ghouls, the fabricated monsters of the Shelleys—it is pretty tame stuff, when it is not actually ludicrous.

De Quincey, eschewing fiction, got farther: his writings on Charles Lloyd's madness, or the orphans of Blentarn Ghyl, or his own opium-taking are more terrible than anything in the poets. And yet his studies of the *summum malum* of horror—murder itself—leave, I think, something to be desired. Among the English authors of his century, De Quincey was the master scribe of murder, but he had the misfortune to live before the appearance of the century's master killer. It is as though Tacitus had lived before Nero, or Burke had died on the eve of the fall of the Bastille.

The discovery of the body of Mary Ann "Polly" Nichols in Buck's Row, Whitechapel, early in the morning of August 31, 1888, seemed, to an untrained eye, to herald the appearance of something new under the sun, a previously unsuspected species of evil. "At a quarter to four o'clock" that morning, says the writer for *The Times*, "Police Constable Neill, 97 J, when in Buck's Row, Whitechapel, came upon the body of a woman lying on a part of the footway." On "stooping to raise her up in the belief that she was drunk, he discovered that her throat was cut almost from ear to ear." Dr. Llewellyn, summoned from his surgery in Whitechapel Road, "discovered that, besides the gash across the throat," the woman had suffered "terrible wounds in the abdomen." The police ambulance came, and the body was taken to Bethnal Green Police Station, where a "further examination showed the horrible nature of the crime, there being other fearful cuts and gashes, any one of which was sufficient to cause death apart from the wounds across the throat."

It was the first of a series of murders which, in their overripe malignity, threw those of the century's other killers into the shade. The consummate figure had appeared; but there was no scholar to do justice to his deviltry.

———•———

To be sure, the time was ripe for his appearance. London had once been a city of parishes, of little cities within the big one, each with its own highly developed protocols of soul-care. In its pastoral prime, in the high mediaeval city, the parish bore responsibility for the souls of its flock; the phrase "lost lamb" was not yet a sentimentality. But an influx of newcomers overwhelmed the old social architecture, and by the nineteenth century it had broken down. It was replaced by a modern police system, one that cared less for saving souls than solving crimes; the wheels of its machines began to turn only *after* the sick soul had done something morbid. Nor did the police have any notion of the particular kinds of soul-sickness which were growing ever more prevalent in the metropolis. De Quincey, working imaginatively on opium, had compiled, in "Three Memorable Murders," a kind of dossier on the nature of the mass killer, a résumé of his attributes; and Krafft-Ebing's *Psychopathia Sexualis*, which appeared in 1886, had supplemented his findings with a wealth of new detail. But neither work had penetrated the consciousness of the police, or indeed of the public.

Anyone today who rummages about the files of Victorian newspapers will see that other artists were working in the same macabre line as the Whitechapel killer, and anticipated his methods. But their significance was overlooked, not only by the police, but by the English clerisy as a whole, by the writers, politicians, and civil servants who directed the intellectual gabble of the age. The clouds had long been gathering on the horizon; but with the exception, perhaps, of a few souls such as Mr. Ruskin, none had recognized in them the portents of the coming storm.

CHAPTER EIGHT

A Weight of Incubus

unrecognized compulsions of my being
—*Ralph Ellison*

S t. Giles's in the 1860s was as vile as ever, and George Street in particular was "one of the worst neighborhoods in the metropolis." Beasts of prey pursued their courses for the most part unmolested by authority, although on occasion they were brought to justice. In 1861 there was a notorious incident in George Street in which a cab-driver, according to *The Times*, attempted "to get a young woman who had been his fare into one of the brothels there." He first "hocused" her—stupefied her with drugs—and afterwards stripped her naked. But in "consequence of the resistance offered by the person who was in charge of the house," the cabman was "prevented from carrying out the worst part of his design," and was captured, tried, and convicted.

Two years later, in April 1863, another young woman found herself in George Street. Emma Jackson was not a typical "unfortunate." She had a home and a family; she lived with her mother, a shirt-maker, and her father, an unemployed clerk, in Berwick Street, Soho. Twenty-eight years old, she was said to be of a "quiet, peaceable" disposition, though given to occasional "fits of irregularity." She would "remain at home for weeks working hard" at her shirts, one of her girlfriends recalled, and "conducting herself reputably," but then she would "break out." She would leave home for days together and "go with anybody."

Around seven o'clock on the morning of Thursday, April 9, 1863, Emma Jackson was seen on the doorstep of No. 4 George Street. With her was a man in his late twenties, in a dark coat and dark trousers. He stood about five foot seven and was fair-haired; he wore a wideawake hat and had small, rather sunken eyes.

No. 4 George Street was one of those houses which "took in people at all hours, without inquiry as to their characters." As Emma Jackson and her man came in, another couple was going out. The servant girl, Martha Curley, showed them to the back room on the first floor; the man gave her a shilling for her pains.

The couple hired the room for the morning only, but noon came and went with no sign of them. Sometime between four and five o'clock, Miss Curley told the under-servant, Catharine Mulind, to go upstairs and "find out why the parties had not left the room." On entering it, Miss Mulind found it streaming with blood; the "bed was saturated and the walls spattered" with it. Emma Jackson lay on her back on the bed with the staring eyes of death. She "only had on her chemise," which "was turned low below the breasts." Her neck and hair were "a mass of congealed blood." Her throat had been "frightfully cut," and the internal jugular vein severed; she had suffered a number of puncture wounds, and on the back of her neck were "two large stabs running obliquely towards each other." On her "left buttock was a mark of the grasp of two fingers," and the window was open.

Miss Jackson's father and brother were summoned to identify the body; and one of her girlfriends told the police that she had seen Emma that morning "in the company of a foreigner, who was having his boots cleaned at the corner of Greek Street* and Compton Street."

——•——

The murder in George Street caused a momentary sensation, and was as quickly forgotten. The killer embodied a type already recognizable in Victorian England, but one that neither the police nor the writers for the press had learned to recognize. Confronted with the coroner's opinion that "no intercourse had taken place," a police detective today would ask himself whether the killer did not nurse a grievance of some kind, perhaps a sexual one. He would note that he wielded the knife with a ferocity out of proportion to the object merely of extinguishing life. He would ask himself what sort of hatred could have driven a man to such an act, and what sort of morbid satisfaction he might have derived from it. Mindful of the admonition that a man with a taste for "unnatural luxury" does not "relapse into inertia," the detective would be quick to consult his own files and those of the police in other cities. Had the man struck before in another port? Was he likely to strike again? But in 1863, police detectives did not ask themselves these questions.

---

* Readers of the *Confessions of an English Opium-Eater* will remember that Greek Street was one of De Quincey's old haunts.

CHAPTER NINE

Unnatural Conjunctions

Tiresias being blind on earth sees more than all
the rest in hell.

—*Sir Thomas Browne*

I t must be admitted that, where murder is concerned,
De Quincey himself was only intermittently a sensitive oracle.
He overlooked entirely the nasty yet illuminative murder
that took place in December 1827 at Oxford, in the shadow of the
domes and spires of the university. It was a place De Quincey knew
well, for as a young scholar he had passed several unsatisfactory
years among its towers and cloisters, breathing "the soft vapours
of a thousand years of learning." He might, indeed, deplore the
limitations of Oxford as an instructress of the young, but he would
surely have acknowledged her virtues as a theater of evil. The commission of an act of the utmost savagery in a place where so much
civilization had long been concentrated—a place practically devoted

to softening the ruder excrescences of barbarism—makes for a collision of worlds, a smashup not only dramatic in itself, but one that throws into the sharpest relief the particular evil in question.

The day—it was Thursday, December 6, 1827—was fine; but as darkness came on, the temperature fell to freezing. Ann Priest, a young woman of twenty-four, was walking with a companion, Harriet Mitchell. Miss Priest was a girl of "great personal beauty," but one who under a load of misfortune had yielded her maidenhood and sunk into the character of an unfortunate; her friend Miss Mitchell was, in this respect, not less compromised. They went down the High Street. Perhaps they passed Gibbon's college, the indolence of whose fellows—the "monks of Magdalene," steeped in port and prejudice—the historian of the Roman Empire had memorably deplored. At all events, they came eventually to Brasenose, the college of the "brazen nose," its name derived from the bronze knocker that once adorned its portal. There they saw, through undraped windows, what must always be an agreeable sight on a December night, candle-lit merry-making in a warm room. A drinking party was under way in the rooms of one of the undergraduates of the college. The young collegians were jolly, and in an access of boisterousness they called out to the two young women, who promptly came to the window. Might not the good fellows give them some wine? Alas, replied a young man, there was no wine; but he should be happy to give them brandy, if they would drink it.

He was twenty years old, this hospitable young man, and he occupied a station in life widely different from that of the young women to whom he now ministered. His name was Houstonne John Radcliffe, and he had high connections amongst the gentry, baronetage, and clergy of England. His grandfather, the Venerable Houstonne Radcliffe, had been Archdeacon of Canterbury, a position of splendor in the English Church; and as if this were not enough, he had also been Subdean of Wells, Prebendary of Ely, and the master of a number of other richly beneficed livings. The young man's father, the Rev. John Radcliffe, had been a fellow of Brasenose, and was now Rector of St. Anne's Limehouse, a pretty Hawksmoor church in London. As for his mother, she was the former Miss Anne Leigh, cousin of Sir Roger Holt Leigh, Baronet. In July the young man's sister, Anne, married the diplomat Sir John-Frederick Croft, Baronet, of Dodington, Kent, and the particular friend of Sir Joseph Banks, botanically illustrious.* A formidable family, young Houstonne's, and highly respectable in clerico-gentry circles, with so many fat livings and eminent relations to their credit—the sort of people who would have been at home in the world of Trollope's Dean Arabin and his Archdeacon Grantly.

The young women were pleased to accept the young gentleman's offer of brandy. But the windows of the young man's rooms were grated with iron, which prevented the passage of glass or bottle. Houstonne John Radcliffe, exhibiting something of the dexterity which had enabled his grandpapa to accumulate, in the rapacious race for Anglican patronage, so many opulent livings, ingeniously overcame the difficulty. He poured the brandy into a teapot, and stuck the spout between the bars. The young women applied their lips to the protrudant instrument and drank deeply of its precious elixir.

What happened afterwards is not clear, but at a quarter past midnight Miss Priest was found in Blue Boar Street, a narrow alley perhaps two hundred yards from the southwestern-most extremity of Brasenose, but rather closer to the still more august precincts of Christ Church, *primus inter pares* among the colleges of Oxford. A man named Hedges, a porter of All Souls, was coming off duty when he found Miss Priest "slumped unconscious in the doorway of his house" in Blue Boar Street. Various watchmen and bystanders offered their assistance, and there was talk of taking Miss Priest away to safety in a barrow; but in the end nothing was done.

---

* John Radcliffe afterwards became Vicar of Dodington and Teynham, and likely delegated his duties as Rector of Limehouse to a curate.

Some time after "Tom," the bell of Christ Church, struck two, a watchman named James Cox found Miss Priest bleeding. He and two other watchmen brought her to the nearest apothecary, who told them she must be taken to the hospital. The watchmen instead took her to her lodgings, where they left her in the care of her landlady, Mrs. Cox. Mrs. Cox, under the impression that the girl was not seriously hurt, "laid her on some blankets in front of the fire to sober up" and went to bed. It was only later, when she examined Miss Priest with a lantern, that she discovered that the girl "was bleeding heavily from her 'woman's parts.'"

Ann Priest died later that day of the injuries she had sustained in the night. She had been cruelly and unusually violated. De Quincey, had he interested himself in the case, might have extracted from it the last drop of terror. The girl was a sympathetic victim, for although poor and fallen, she was beautiful: after viewing her body at the inquest, the jurors, who had returned a verdict of murder by a person or persons unknown, agreed that she was "the most handsome" woman "they had ever seen," with the "most perfect symmetry and delicacy of limbs." De Quincey, who candidly acknowledged his own opium addiction, was not one to shrink from scandal, but he might well have quailed before details which, even if relegated to the decent obscurity of a learned language, were shockingly obscene. The bruises to Miss Priest's "left breast, which were believed to have been caused by pressure from four fingers and the thumb of a man's hand," he might have recorded with comparative equanimity; but the outrage to her womanhood was something else altogether.

———•———

The human fiend or fiends who mutilated Ann Priest were never punished. A house painter, John Williams, was charged with the crime, but the evidence against him was slight, and the grand jury declined to find a true bill. Houstonne John Radcliffe confessed to having given Miss Priest brandy on the last night of her life, and he was formally "sent down" by his college the following month, in January 1828, it being understood that he was free to return to Brasenose after the summer or "long" vacation. Houstonne, however, declined to avail himself of this privilege, and indeed he left Oxford before the decision was handed down. He never returned. He died, in the autumn of 1829, at the age of twenty-two, in the house of his aunt, Mrs. Pemberton, in Spring Garden Terrace, London. Curiously enough, his name is not inscribed in the pages of *The Radcliffes of Leigh Lancashire, A Family Memorial.* The reader who takes the trouble to examine that obscure volume will find the names of his two sisters duly set down, together with those of their clerical and diplomatic husbands—but he will search in vain for that of Houstonne; it is as though he had never been.

Whig Murder

prosaical rogues

—*Dr. Johnson*

T he Ripper had other forerunners. On May 6, 1838, Eliza Grimwood, who worked as a prostitute in the West End, was found murdered in a room at 2 Wellington Terrace, Lambeth. She had been stabbed twice in the neck and throat, and after her body "had been divested of the clothes in which it was enveloped," as the writer for *The Times* put it, it was found that "she had received a severe wound a little above the nipple of the left breast," and two other deep wounds in the abdomen, all of which "were no doubt inflicted by a sharp-pointed instrument," for her "outward dress and also her stays, which were made of a very strong material," had been cut through.

On March 26, 1841, Elizabeth Winks, a woman of thirty-six with "very creditable connexions," was found near death on the grass at the end of a lane in the London suburb of Norwood. It "was evident that the unfortunate woman had been brutally maltreated," as her clothes "were dragged nearly over her head," and there "were appearances of severe bruises about her person." She afterwards died of her injuries. On January 18, 1843, the body of a woman, mutilated and burned, was fished out of the river Aire in Liverpool. On January 6, 1845, the body of a well-dressed woman in her early twenties, Emma Ashburnham, was discovered dead in the mud of the Thames near the steps of Waterloo Bridge; a "dreadful wound," of "considerable depth," had been inflicted upon her in the vicinity of the left hip-bone.

If none of these murders lives in the imagination of history, it is partly because they were recorded by inferior scribes. The "common reporter," says a character in Arthur Machen's novel *The Inmost Light*, "is a dull dog; every story he has to tell is spoilt in the telling. His idea of horror and what excites horror is so lamentably deficient." At the same time, the crueler sorts of crimes were becoming more common; murders far more gruesome than Thurtell's of Weare excited nothing like as much popular revulsion, and were instead shrugged off as a fact of metropolitan life.

There is another reason why the crimes left short smart upon the collective psyche. Murder was coming to be looked at in a new way. Once it had been conceived as a demonic act, with mysterious springs in the reptilian depths of the soul. But in the age of Victoria, it was being rationalized into a social fact, with its ultimate cause in the material circumstances of the murderer's life. The word "conditions" had come into vogue. By "conditions" was meant the various antecedent causes that contribute to particular results. The great thing about "conditions" is that they could be studied empirically, by means of the social and natural sciences. Moreover, they could be remedied politically, through social legislation. Murder, in the new theory—the Whig theory—differed from bad drains and inadequate plumbing in degree but not in kind; it, too, could be alleviated by Acts of Parliament. The criminal, it was pointed out, had had a hard childhood; had lived unhygienically; had been fed an unsatisfactory diet; was insufficiently educated. Alter the conditions, and you would have fewer criminals.

The Whig theory of crime was sound, so far as it went; the vital statistics have long shown that in hard times, the number of certain kinds of crime (housebreaking, larceny, embezzlement) goes up. The trouble with the Whig theory is that in good times, the number of depraved crimes does not go down. Since the reign of Victoria, countless slums have been cleared and social welfare programs instituted; the poor, in Europe and America today, enjoy luxuries unknown to the rich of a century ago; and obesity has replaced hunger as the curse of the lower classes. Yet mass murders have become as innumerable as the leaves of Vallombrosa. Like cancer and mental depression, the phenomenon of the psychopath appears to be one of those malignancies which flourishes most abundantly in the sunshine of progress and enlightenment.

CHAPTER ELEVEN

The Trivialization of Evil

For it is here that Fantasy with her mystic wonder-
land plays into the small prose domain of Sense,
and becomes incorporated therewith. In the Symbol
proper, what we can call a Symbol, there is ever,
more or less distinctly and directly, some embodi-
ment and revelation of the Infinite. . . .

—Thomas Carlyle

Plato spoke in figures, for he saw many things with
the light of his mind which he could not express
in words.

—Dante (to Con Grande)

The *Times*, June 7, 1865. The body of an unknown woman,
aged about thirty-five, is fished up naked from the Thames.
The Times, December 17, 1872. On Christmas Day, the body

of a "good-looking girl" in her twenties is discovered dead in her room in 12 Great Corham Street, Bloomsbury, with "a wound on the left of the wind-pipe large enough to put a man's fist in"; she is identified as Harriet Buswell, also known as Clara Bruton, a dancer in the Alhambra, the music hall in Leicester Square. *The Times*, September 20, 1873. Police continue their unavailing efforts to trace the murderer of a woman whose mutilated and dismembered body has been found, piece by piece, in the Thames. The left quarter of the trunk was discovered on September 5 in the river-mire near Battersea Waterworks, where, afterwards, the left thigh and the breasts were also recovered. On September 6, the face and scalp (which had been detached from the skull) surfaced off Limehouse; the nose had been cut away from the face and hung by a shred of flesh from the upper lip. The legs were found at Lambeth; one of the feet by the mouth of the Surrey Canal; an arm near the Albert Embankment; the right thigh and a portion of the pelvis at Woolwich Arsenal; a shoulder near Greenwich; and the left forearm at the Albert Bridge.

————•————

Even in the heyday of the cult of progress, it was obvious to some observers that the certain kinds of mental and spiritual debility could not be entirely explained by reference to the price of corn or fluctuations in the cattle market, to the quality of the sewers or the state of the poor laws. Krafft-Ebing was among the first researchers to study depraved homicides in the light of medicine and psychology; and today his work is carried on by researchers in the fields of genetics and neurochemistry. Such studies are, of course, valuable; but like their counter-studies in the social sciences, they have had the effect of diminishing the evilness of evil.

Evil loses a good deal of its horror when you succumb to the illusion that it can be done away with by means of better plumbing or a saving pill, the establishment of a more intelligent school curriculum or a reformation of the gene pool. The more one gets into the habit of thinking of evil as a byproduct of social or economic circumstances, or as an anomaly in the neural architecture of the brain, the harder it becomes for one to take it seriously as a permanent element in the soul, one's own included. The first principle of goodness, it would seem, is to accord evil a healthy respect.

De Quincey, a Tory of the old school, anticipated the psychological insights of Krafft-Ebing and discerned as clearly as any up-to-date Whig the element of monstrous sexuality in the character of the psycho. But he never lost sight of the residuum of mystery that remains after science has done its best to account for the degeneracy; never ceased to be conscious of the deeper spiritual horror of particular crimes, the diabolic imponderable which never will be apprehended by empirical science, or explained in crude prose.* Evil, if it be really evil, has in it something of the shadowy and indistinct. It is enveloped in an obscurity which the poet or the prophet may partly penetrate, but which the light of reason and science can never wholly dispel. There is that in it which "passeth understanding." The rational or empirical investigator affects to solve the mystery of a particular evil when he has in fact but grazed the surface of its horror; it is as though he had lit a candle and, pleased with the little circle of illumination he had made, flattered himself that he had vanquished darkness.

---·---

* As much as Thoreau, De Quincey believed that there is "a chasm between knowledge and ignorance which the arches of science can never span." The same conclusion was reached by the physicist Max Planck. Having devoted, he said, "his whole life to the most clear-headed science, to the study of matter," he concluded that science "cannot solve the ultimate mystery of nature. And that is because, in the last analysis, we ourselves are part of nature and therefore part of the mystery that we are trying to solve." The solution to the ultimate mystery of evil is perhaps no less elusive.

The Times, March 11, 1879. A white deal box is found floating in the Thames and, when opened, proves to contain pieces of a young woman's body, each of them wrapped in brown paper. *The Times,* June 5, 1880. The decomposing body of an unknown woman is found in a cask covered with chloride of lime in the cellar of a house in Harley Street. *The Times,* March 11, 1884. The body of a woman in her twenties, Mary Ann ("Annie") Yates, is discovered around noon on Sunday, March 9, in her room in 12 Burton Crescent. She lay on the bed partially undressed under the bedclothes, with her head resting on the pillow in a pool of blood. There was a "serious gash" on the left side of her head, and the towel that covered her mouth had been tied round the back of her head. Around three o'clock that morning, a man and woman in the next room had been awakened by screams coming from Miss Yates's room, "but no notice was taken of the circumstance," as Miss Yates "was subject to fits of hysteria, and frequently made similar noises." *The Times,* July 13, 1887. An inquiry is opened in connection with a pair of human legs and human arms found wrapped in canvas in the Regent's Canal on June 30. They were thought to belong to a human trunk which was discovered sewn up in canvas in the Thames near Rainham Creek on May 11. The trunk, on examination, appeared to be that of a woman in her twenties: the "internal organs were missing" from it, the "spine had been sawn through," and the "thighs had been taken out at the sockets." The trunk corresponded to the chest and thorax of a woman found in the Thames at Temple Pier on June 5: the collarbone and breasts "had been taken off," but the "lungs were present." The head of the woman was never found, nor was the identity of the killer ever discovered.

CHAPTER TWELVE

The Lesson of the Master

Hell is naked before God.

—Symmachus

Surely it is no coincidence that at the very moment when murder was being degraded into a socio-medical problem, to be alleviated by Acts of Parliament, it was simultaneously being trivialized into a form of light entertainment, the literary equivalent of a parlor game. The detective story, which grew to maturity during the reign of Victoria, begins, as a rule, with an instance of mysterious crime or terror, quite as unfathomable as De Quincey's Wapping murders. The terror seems at first to partake of the weirdness of nightmare and the occult; it is bound up with an infernal hound, or a Peruvian vampire, or a man with a yellow face. But by degrees the mysterious mists are dissolved by the genial light of deductive logic, which it is the role of the detective (the hero of the story) to supply; and in the end the reader discovers that the hound of hellish aspect is in fact an ordinary canine got up with phosphorus by an all-too-human villain.

The trick of transmuting an apparently infernal mystery into a merely rational one is not easily mastered, and in time writers of detective novels found that they need not master it. Their readers, they discovered, wanted nothing so much as to pass a few idle hours in as mentally unstimulating a way as possible. The main thing, then, was to get the first victim killed as rapidly and efficiently as possible, for only then could the guessing game (the chief pleasure of a detective novel) begin. The element of palpable evil is all but absent in these books; in its place we find a drawing-room comedy of butlers, vicars, dowagers, and retired colonels, phrased in an ironic-genteel prose such as Jane Austen might have written had she been drawn to empty subjects.*

It is true that, as detective fiction grew more tepidly mannered, readers hungry for gore—for "rawhead and bloody bones"—became impatient. The thriller came to market. But the thriller has proved a difficult genre to sustain; authors are obliged to compete with one another to devise ever more improbable and outré forms of the grotesque, which they proceed to describe in painstaking detail. But just as there is beggary in the love that can be reckoned, so there is banality in the horror that is too ingenuously transcribed. When an author leaves the precise nature of the evil he is conjuring ambiguous, as Henry James does in *The Turn of the Screw*, the imagination

---

* Sherlock Holmes, T. S. Eliot writes, "was deceiving Watson when he told him that he had bought his Stradivarius violin for a few shillings at a second-hand shop in the Tottenham Court Road. He found that violin in the ruins of the house of Usher." Perhaps; but Poe must not be blamed for the inanities of the detective fiction his work inspired. "Robbery and murder have degenerated into Chinese puzzles," Charles Whibley says of the detective novel, "whose solution is a pleasant irritant to the idle brain. The misunderstanding of Poe has produced a vast polyglot literature, for which one would not give in exchange a single chapter of Captain Smith [an old writer of Newgate lives]. Vautrin and Bill Sykes are already discredited, and it is a false reflection of M. Dupin, which dazzles the eye of a moral and unimaginative world."

of the reader cooperates with the language of the writer to fill up the cup of horror. But when, in a book like Bret Easton Ellis's *American Psycho*, written a century later, the light is too naïvely bright, the result is not horror, but something ludicrous and *bouffe*, and incapable of affording either amusement or instruction.

———•———

While authors in the West End of London were busy contriving unreal stories in which genteel personages were being elegantly slaughtered in rural vicarages, in the East End real women were being murdered with every circumstance of degradation and horror.

No one who was living in London in the autumn of 1888, says Sir Melville Macnaghten, who afterwards rose to be Assistant Commissioner of the Metropolitan Police, "will forget the terror created by these murders. Even now I can recall the foggy evenings, and hear again the raucous cries of the newspaper boys: '*Another horrible murder, murder, mutilation, Whitechapel.*' Such was the burden of their ghastly song; and, when the double murder of 30 September took place, the exasperation of the public at the non-discovery of the perpetrator knew no bounds, and no servant-maid deemed her life safe if she ventured out to post a letter after ten o'clock at night."

Sir Melville is as good a guide as any to the way in which the Whitechapel murders were perceived by those who followed them at the time. He supposes (as many Ripper authorities still do) that the first "real" Whitechapel murder was that which took the life of Mary Ann Nichols, who was found in Bucks Row in the early hours of August 31 "with her throat cut and her body slightly mutilated."*

---

* On April 3, 1888, more than four months before the first of the "canonical" murders, Emma Smith was found "horribly outraged" in Osborne Street; she afterwards died in the London Hospital. On August 7, Martha Tabram was discovered dead in George Yard. Her throat had been cut, and she had sustained a number of wounds in the chest and abdomen. But neither victim seems have been mutilated in the way all but one of the "canonical" five were.

Nine days later, the body of Annie Chapman was discovered behind a house in Hanbury Street; her throat had been cut in the same manner as Nichols's, but she had sustained, Sir Melville writes, mutilations of "a much more savage character."

On September 27, the notorious "Dear Boss" letter, signed "Jack the Ripper," was received in that rather louche bureau of public intelligence, the Central News Agency in the Strand. Professing to be "down on whores," the writer made a vow: *I shant quit ripping them till I do get buckled.*" Sir Melville detects in the letter "the stained forefinger of the journalist," and he supposes it to have been the work of a newspaper-man intent on fabricating sensational copy. The letter soon became public knowledge, and many Londoners who (like the authorities themselves) believed it to be genuine were wrought up to a new pitch of fear and indignation.

Just as the Ripper legend was taking form, the infamous "double event" occurred: two murders which were committed within a short time of each other on September 30. Elizabeth Stride was found in Berners Street with her throat cut; she had not, however, been mutilated. This, Sir Melville surmises, was because "the murderer was disturbed at his demoniacal work by some Jews who at that hour drove up to an anarchist club in the street." The killer's thirst for blood unslaked, he "started off in search of another victim, whom he found in Catherine Eddowes." Her "body, very badly mutilated," was discovered "in a dark corner of Mitre Square."

There followed a respite of forty days and forty nights, during which the frenzy of the public gradually died down, only to be fear-fully revived when, on the morning of November 9, the mutilated corpse of Mary Jane Kelly was found in her room in 13 Miller's Court. She was, Sir Melville writes, a "comparatively young woman of some twenty-five years of age," and was "said to have been pos-sessed of considerable personal attractions." On the last night of her life, she entertained several men in her room, and was heard to sing a popular song, "A Violet from Mother's Grave." Her murder, Sir Melville writes, was "the last of the series, and it was by far the most horrible." The mutilations "were of a positively fiendish description, almost indescribable in their savagery, and the doctors who were called in to examine the remains averred that the operator must have been at least two hours over his hellish job. A fire was burning low in the room, but neither candles nor gas were there. The madman made a bonfire of some old newspapers, and of his victim's clothes, and, by this dim, irreligious light, a scene was enacted which nothing seen by Dante in his visit to the infernal regions could have surpassed."*

Whatever Sir Melville's virtues as a cicerone, it is his limitations and blindnesses that are most palpable. Where are the swirling fogs and lurid, gaslit alleys of the metropolitan Maleboge? Where are the crowds of the undernourished and unemployed standing about in the streets in a "dull, aimless, discouraged way," "too apathetic to move"? Where are the fallen women who filled the squalid lodging houses, resignedly or drunkenly practicing the saddest of professions? Where is the erotic cannibal himself? Sir Melville is probably right when he says that "the fury of the murderer, as evinced in his methods of mutilation, increased on every occasion," and that "his appetite appears to have become sharpened by indulgence." (He who has a taste for "unnatural luxury" does not "relapse into inertia.") But although Sir Melville recognizes that

---

* Dr. J. R. Gabe, who examined the body of Miss Kelly in Miller's Court, said that "in all his experience in dissecting-rooms he never had seen such ghastliness. The corpse was found nearly naked, on a blood-engorged woolen mattress. The victim's hair was flung upward on a pillow and matted with gore. The fingers, nose and ears were sliced away. The throat was cut from left to right. Below the neck was the appearance such as the carcass of a sheep presents in an abattoir, with the ribs and back-bone exposed and cleared of the stomach, entrails, heart, and liver. These organs were placed carefully beside the mutilated trunk, after the fashion in a butcher shop. As on previous occasions the uterus and ovarian adjuncts were missing. The flesh on each side of a cut on the median line was carefully folded an inch or two away from the cut. From the hips to the ankles the flesh was shredded more or less. It must have been the work of perhaps a full half-hour, said the physician. Both her breasts, too, had been cut clean away and placed by the side of her liver and other organs on the table."

CHAPTER THIRTEEN

The Vital Lamp

From shadowy types to truth

—*Milton*

U nlike the slaughter in Wapping, the Whitechapel murders
inspired no work of literary art in which their horrors
were recreated through the power of a master. Yet the
murders nevertheless made an impression on English literature,
or rather on that part of it which was true to the old Tory theory
of evil, which held that the best way to understand the horrors of
the present is to study them in the light of the poetries of the past.

The Whig theory of evil, which reduced it to a problem of social
hygiene, had come to dominate European letters in the nineteenth
century, as it did nearly every other department of life. It found
its most articulate expression in the realism or naturalism of such
writers as Gissing and Zola, who were "quite sure that the soul is a
nervous fluid." But there were always writers, both in England and

on the Continent, who were faithful to the older methods. Balzac's Vautrin, under a semblance of realistic portraiture, is an infernal fiend, with this additional distinction, that as a character he is not unsympathetic and is for that reason the more disturbing. The character that is *wholly* evil disturbs no one's self-complacency, precisely because few people think of themselves as wholly bad and therefore see no connection between themselves and the villain they read about; they fail to see that the worst people differ from the best only in degree.

Dostoevsky (who incidentally admired De Quincey and thought of translating him) wrote the two best murder mysteries of the century; but the murders in *Crime and Punishment* and *The Brothers Karamazov* are solved, not with the detective's magnifying glass or an appeal for reform legislation, but through the author's understanding of the struggle between good and evil that is continuously taking place in the human soul, which he depicts as a contest between the philosophies of Christ and Anti-Christ.

———•———

I find, in the works of certain writers who lived through the Whitechapel murders, passages that conjure precisely the *fiendishness* which is the dominant note of the Ripper, and do so in a language closely related to the old Gothic rhetorics of diabolism. Henry James fled to the Continent, he told his brother William, to get "away from Whitechapel" and the "hundred other constantly thickening heavinesses" that oppressed him during the "detestable summer" of 1888. A decade later, he conjured a similarly mysterious evil in *The Turn of the Screw,* in which two children are the victims of an "infernal" ghoulishness. Only it is never clear whether the governess who tells the story is doing her best to protect the children from the lurking evil, or whether she is herself the ghoulish being, the parasitic vampire, who preys upon them in the insane belief that she is saving them from perdition.

The fiendishness of Whitechapel has its echo, too, in certain of the characters of Joseph Conrad, most notably "Mr. Jones," the living ghoul in *Victory*, and Mr. Kurtz, the cannibal anti-hero of *Heart of Darkness*. On going back, just now, to *Victory*, I find that Conrad has drawn so copiously on the Gothic idioms that I wonder whether he has not perhaps overdone it. The "dark, sunken stare" of Mr. Jones, the misogynist villain of the book, is that of "an incurious spectre"; and his voice "somehow matched his sunken eyes." It is "hollow" and "distant," as though spoken "from the bottom of a well." His "handsome but emaciated face" is corpse-like, and the "spectral intensity" of his glance has the power to "dissolve the last grain of resolution" in the man upon whom he chooses to fix it. His "lifeless manner" seems "to imply some sort of menace from beyond the grave" and a mastery of "horrors worse than murder." He resembles nothing so much as an "insolent spectre on leave from Hades, endowed with skin and bones and a subtle power of terror." Conrad has laid it on pretty thick; but it must be remembered that I have here gathered in one place descriptions which in the book itself are spread out over the course of many pages. So dispersed, they are, I think, entirely effective.

The Decay of Murder

> I believe that all minds which have contemplated
> such horrors as deeply as I have done, must, for
> their own protection from utter despondency,
> have early encouraged and cherished some tran-
> quillising belief as to the future balances and the
> hieroglyphic meanings of human sufferings.
>
> —De Quincey

The Ripper murders were an instance of the evil De Quincey diagnosed in his essay on the Wapping murders—the evil of the erotic cannibal, the modern serial killer. But although the evil had taken root in England long before the Ripper himself struck, the Victorian mind was unfit to comprehend it and was therefore taken by surprise by the carnage in East London in 1888. De Quincey, had he been living at that hour, might have written something that did justice to the Gothic psychology of the

Whitechapel murderer: no contemporary writer did. The Romantic wave had crested.

And yet there was at least one Victorian literary man who, where murder was concerned, saw a little farther than his contemporaries. Quite as much as De Quincey, Leslie Stephen* deplored the trivialization of murder. De Quincey, in his 1827 essay "On Murder Considered as One of the Fine Arts," mocked the shallowness of the modern attitude toward homicide; he imagined a "Society of Connoisseurs in Murder" whose members professed "to be curious in homicide; amateurs and dilettanti in the various modes of carnage; and, in short, Murder-Fanciers. Every fresh atrocity of that class which the police annals of Europe bring up, they meet and criticise as they would a picture, statue, or other work of art." In a similar vein, Stephen, in his 1869 essay "The Decay of Murder," lamented the disintegration of sensibility which was coarsening the modern perception of murder. No "power of imaginative insight" was, he said, being brought to bear on the subject; and as evidence of the degeneration, he pointed to the rise of the modern detective novel. The murder mystery, he said, had become "a weariness to the flesh," and the "intelligent detective" a "drug in the market."

It was not that Stephen objected to murder literature per se. "If all novels and dramas turning upon startling crimes were to be expunged from our literature," he wrote, "we should have to make a surprisingly clean sweep. *Hamlet* and *Othello* and *King Lear* would have to go at once; Richardson's great novel would be put into the critic's *Index*; even Sir Walter Scott would require expurgation. . . ." What Stephen regretted was the loss of grandeur in murder writing. The infernal mystery inherent in the act of one man deliberately doing another to death without the justification of war, self-defense, the executioner's writ, or the code duello, was

---

* Afterwards Sir Leslie, Knight Commander of the Bath; father of Virginia Woolf.

being lost in the pleasant whimsies of the *whodunit*; the spirit of Wilkie Collins and Paul Féval was coming to prevail over that of De Quincey.

Quite true; only Stephen was less satisfactory in explaining *why* the Victorians wrote murder's epitaph. Like De Quincey before him, he fingered, as his scapegoat, Progress, that mysterious force which, he said, was "insidiously transforming us into a very dull, highly respectable, and intensely monotonous collection of insignificant units." But he failed to isolate the particular strain of dullness which had proved so fatal to murder. As a "Godless Victorian," Stephen could not, perhaps, bring himself to admit it, but the dullness he lamented was that of a people too engrossed in their day-to-day material well-being to rise to the *spiritual* apprehension of evil.*

"Poetry" is an ambiguous word; where murder is concerned, it is enough to say that it is a means of describing experience that lies beyond the literal reality to which our commonplace language refers. The poet cannot, of course, forego the use of this everyday language when he invokes these inarticulable aspects of our being; but precisely because he is trying to describe not only the "real" world which the senses apprehend but another world that is *not* present to the senses, he resorts to a language of metaphors and symbols, to what we call poetry.

---

* In his essay "Witches, and Other Night Fears," Lamb argues that the night-evils we dread are often metaphysical rather than physical in nature: "the kind of fear here treated of is purely spiritual . . . it is strong in proportion as it is objectless on earth." Such fear, he speculates, may "afford some probable insight into our ante-mundane existence, and a peep at least into the shadow-land of pre-existence." The devils of our nightmares are for Lamb a symbolic expression of our terror before the incomprehesibility of a universe bounded by such enigmatical propositions as Eternity and Infinity.

It was the achievement of De Quincey to see that, if a writer was to get his hands around a thing like murder—if he was to do justice to it in the way Shakespeare did justice to it in *Macbeth*—he could not very well do without this poetic and figurative language. It was for this reason that, although he himself wrote prose and not verse, he drew freely, in his murder writings, on the language of the poets, which he used to make his reader sensible of murder's Gothic depths, abysses which more pedestrian writers overlooked.

———•———

Much like Stephen and De Quincey, the twentieth-century critic Edmund Wilson blamed progress for the banalization of murder. In his essay "Why Do People Read Detective Stories?"—one of three he wrote on that vacuous genre—he argued that progress has at once subjected men to new kinds of uncertainty and at the same time undermined the credibility of those religious consolations which do something to reconcile people to the precariousness of their situation. The modern man, Wilson wrote, lives in perpetual fear of disaster; yet when disasters come, he is never able "to pin down the responsibility" for them with any degree of certainty. He is demoralized by the feeling that he is surrounded by evil-doers lurking in the shadows, or sitting comfortably in places of power— evil-doers who, moreover, are always getting away with it. For the agitated modern man, the detective novel, Wilson argued, is balm in Gilead: it enables him to forget, for a moment, the complexities and ambiguities of the world in which he lives, and gives him the satisfaction of temporarily inhabiting a make-believe world in which the bad guy (who undoubtedly *is* a bad guy) is always caught and justly punished. The murderer is spotted, Wilson writes, "and—relief!—he is not, after all, a person like you or me. He is a villain—known to the trade as George Gruesome—and he has been caught by an infallible Power, the supercilious and omniscient detective, who knows exactly where to fix the guilt."

It is Wilson's theory that the modern reader adores detective fiction in part because he finds in it a substitute for a lost religion; he is consoled by the presence, in the heart of the mystery novel, of an omniscient God, one who has incarnated himself as an infallible private eye, ever ready to detect and punish the sinning criminal. But if this is true—if the readers of these ersatz gospels really do seek a religious consolation in them—surely there must come a time when they ask themselves why the omniscient detective-divinity is content to punish cartoon villains only. Why is he never shown to prosecute more credible evil-doers than poor George Gruesome, whom he is always running to ground? Why do Agatha Christie and Dorothy Sayers never give their readers the courage to look real evil-doing in the face? The detective novel gives its proselytes not Macbeth or Vautrin, but George Gruesome, and can do no other. For it is very hard to look, closely and steadily, at something that is really appalling (the Moors murders, for example) if you haven't, in the back of your mind, a compensatory idea of goodness to buck you up. A real religion supplies the prophylactic ideal—the vision of transcendent grace that enables those who have embraced it to look closely at evil; he who believes that his redeemer liveth can contemplate even the spider sucking the life-juices out of its victim without feeling that the universe is morally sick.

It is precisely because Shakespeare (I think) believed (or hoped) that there *is* "a divinity that shapes our ends, rough-hew them how we will," that he was able to look so closely not only at Iago, but also at Lear as he carries the body of Cordelia in his arms.* It is the same with the tragic poets of Athens. The Dionysian orgy became Attic tragedy only when Athens itself was Platonizing, moving toward a belief that there is an arch-goodness which is not only stronger

---

* "And if my sensations could add anything to the general suffrage," says Dr. Johnson, "I might relate, I was many years ago so shocked by Cordelia's death, that I know not whether I ever endured to read again the last scenes of the play till I undertook to revise them as an editor."

than evil, but which will eventually overcome it.* Armed with this apotropaic confidence, Aeschylus and Sophocles could look Medusa in the face without fear of her petrifying power. For although Plato had not yet translated, into the language of philosophy, the belief that grace will prevail, the idea was in the air. Aeschylus, certainly, has caught the essence of it when he has the chorus in *Agamemnon* sing of wisdom as the χάρις (a favor, grace, or loveliness of the gods) which comes drop by drop to men through anguish and suffering, that is, through the experience of evil.

With detective fiction, it is different. Having no vision of a greater goodness, the books cannot conjure a deeper horror. Dante could plumb the depths of hell because he knew that Beatrice was in heaven. But Sir Arthur Conan Doyle has no such faith; and that is why Sherlock Holmes, for all the brilliance of his mind, is a lost soul. At a time when all "Europe was ringing with his name," Watson says in "The Adventure of Reigate Square," when "his room was literally ankle-deep with congratulatory telegrams, I found him a prey to the blackest depression."

———•———

With the Ripper murders, the history of Romantic murder which it has been my object to trace comes properly to its end. Already, in 1888, the highly poetic and spiritualized language with which Carlyle and De Quincey sought to understand murder had ceased to be credible; and it is no more so now, in an age which, if it has lost the taste of God, is even more oblivious of the stench of the Devil. The sages of the Enlightenment taught their proselytes to scoff at the old theories of evil which De Quincey and Carlyle sought to revive: reason and science, they believed, would usher in a world

---

* "O goodness infinite, goodness immense! / That all this good of evil shall produce, / And evil turn to good." Milton, *Paradise Lost*, XII, 469–71. Murder can never of course be condoned: yet precisely because it is among the most harrowing forms of evil, it has sometimes driven men to God.

that could do without such Gothic nonsense. That notable merchant of light, Francis Bacon, went so far as to argue that inductive science would prepare the way for a new Eden. It is a belief that is just now in vogue in Silicon Valley, where the cyber moguls are busy planning to live forever, or, failing that, for five hundred years. Carlyle and De Quincey would have blanched at such alchemistical overreaching—shrunk from the shallowness and hubris of it as from a thing but too likely to breed new forms of Gothic horror.

Could it be that they were right to try to rouse us from our prosaic slumbers? Have we not had enough of utopiasts who pretend that we can abolish evils which are inseparable from our nature? If so, the time may be ripe for a reappraisal of the work of the Romantic murder writers.

Acknowledgments

I have especially to thank, in connection with the writing of this book, Michael Carlisle of InkWell Management and Jessica Case of Pegasus. I am, too, deeply grateful to my family for their love and support.

Notes and Sources

xi   *In his essay*: George Orwell, "The Decline of the English Murder," *Tribune*, 15 February 1946.

xiii   *"To move a horror skillfully"*: Charles Lamb, *The Dramatic Essays of Charles Lamb* (London: Chatto & Windus, 1891), 214.

xv   *Sir Robert Walpole*: He was raised to the peerage in 1742 as Earl of Orford.

xvi   *"Charming as were all"*: Jane Austen, *Northanger Abbey* (London: Murray, 1818).

xvii   *"a deeper philosophy"*: John Henry Newman, *Apologia pro vita sua: Being a History of his Religious Opinions* (London: Longmans, Green, 1875), 96.

xvii   *"love—for a person"*: Isaiah Berlin, *Against the Current: Essays in the History of Ideas* (Oxford: Clarendon Press, 1989), 7.

xvii   *"new conquering empire"*: Edmund Burke, *Reflections on the Revolution in France* (London: J. Dodsley, 1791), 114.

xviii   *"He hath a demon"*: William Hazlitt, "On the Living Poets," in Hazlitt, *Lectures on the English Poets* (London: J. M. Dent, 1916), 153. Hazlitt was alluding to the New Testament verses.

xviii   *"flowers that adorn"*: Ibid.

xviii   *"really began to talk ghostly"*: *The Poetical Works of Percy Bysshe Shelley* (London: E. Moxon, 1870), I, lxxxix.

xix   *"suddenly shrieking"*: Ibid.

xx   *"a kind of ghastly object"*: Thomas Carlyle, *Reminiscences* (London: Macmillan, 1887), 293.

xx   *"vampire bats"*: Shelley, "The Triumph of Life," in *The Poetical Works of Percy Bysshe Shelley* (London: Macmillan, 1891), 484.

1   *"This lane is a d—d nasty"*: *The Times*, 31 October 1823.

3   *"That is the place"*: *A Narrative of the Murder of Mr. Weare* (London: J. Edgerley [1824]), 8.

4   *"cold-blooded villainy"*: *The Times*, 31 October 1823.

4   *"dull uniformity"*: The Times, 5 November 1823.

4   *"offer no apology"*: Ibid.

5   most *"literary"* of British murders: Albert Borowitz, *The Thurtell-Hunt Murder Case* (London: Robson, 1988), 254.

7   *"lord of the concourse"*: George Borrow, quoted in "An Historical Villain," *Macmillan's Magazine* (June 1900), LXXXII, 131; see also Borrow, *Lavengro: The Scholar—the Gypsy—the Priest* (London: John Lane, 1902), 169–70.

7   *"were grey"*: Ibid., 154.

7   mastiff's jowl: George Borrow, *Celebrated Trials and Remarkable Cases of Criminal Jurisprudence* (London: Knight and Lacey, 1825), VI, 534.

7   *"a gentleman of fortune"*: The Sporting Magazine (May 1823) (London: Pittman, 1823), XII, 113.

7   *"particularly neat and clean"*: The Fatal Effects of Gambling Exemplified in the Murder of William Weare (London: Thomas Kelly, 1824), xi.

8   *"flattered himself"*: Ibid., xiv.

8   *"Crœsus of the great community of gamesters"*: "Crockford and Crockford's," in *Bentley's Miscellany* (London: Richard Bentley, 1845), XVII, 142.

8   [Thurtell] advertised: Charles Mackie, *Norfolk Annals* (Norwich: Norfolk Chronicle, 1901) I, 190.

9   *"coaxed and dandled"*: Sir Walter Scott, quoted in J. G. Lockhart, *Memoirs of the Life of Sir Walter Scott* (Paris: Baudry's European Library, 1837–38), III, 143. Scott was alluding to Edmund Burke's characterization of the career of the fifth Duke of Bedford.

9   *"having voted, dined, drunk"*: Byron, Don Juan, in *The Complete Works of Lord Byron* (Paris: Galignani, 1831), 615.

9   *"If one could suppose"*: The Creevey Papers (New York: E. P. Dutton, 1904), 422.

9–10   *"Lady Londonderry"*: Ibid.

10   *"so naked"*: The Letters of Horace Walpole (London: Richard Bentley, 1840), II, 270.

10   *"a sharp, cunning, luxurious"*: Charles Greville, quoted in George W. E. Russell, "Lord Beaconsfield's Portrait-Gallery," in *Cornhill Magazine* (January 1907), 30.

10   *"multitudes of the squalid"*: The Tatler, 29 December 1830.

10   *"with the most rank"*: "Report from the Select Committee of the House of Commons, appointed to inquire into the Education of the Lower Orders in the Metropolis," in *The British Review* (London: Hatchard, 1817), IX, 54.

10–11   *"on tiptoe to pay"*: Edward Gibbon Wakefield, *England and America: A Comparison of the Social and Political State of Both Nations* (London: Richard Bentley, 1833), I, 61. Wakefield was an adventurer who attempted to make his fortune by kidnapping an heiress, Ellen Turner of Pott Shrigley; he was sentenced to three years' imprisonment in Newgate for his part in the Shrigley abduction.

11   *"without a single shred"*: Report of the Select Committee of the House of Commons (London: Gale and Fenner, 1816), 451.

13   *"appropriately denominated 'hells'"*: Fatal Effects of Gambling, op. cit., xxi.

13   *"proprietors, or more properly"*: "Gaming-Houses," in *The Westminster Review* (October 1829) (London: Robert Heward *et alia*, 1829), XI, 321.

13   *"a Select Club"*: Ibid., XI, 317.

13   *"as a bait"*: Ibid., XI, 318.

13   *"visit to the French hazard-table"*: Ibid.

13   *"thus allured"*: Ibid.

14   *"extravagant vulgar indulgence"*: George Otto Trevelyan, *The Early History of Charles James Fox* (New York: Harper & Brothers, 1881), 42.

14   *"fine full figure"*: A Narrative of the Mysterious and Dreadful Murder of Mr. W. Weare (London: J. McGowan, n.d.), 90.

14   *"cheap and good"*: Pierce Egan, *Recollections of John Thurtell* (London: Knight & Lacey, 1824), 36.

15   *"a good flat"*: Fatal Effects of Gambling, op. cit, xiv.

15   *"Swell Yokel"*: Ibid.

15   *"even to bull-dog fierceness"*: Pierce Egan, *Boxiana; or, Sketches of Modern Pugilism* (London: G. Virtue, 1829), III, 287.

16   *"exercise and abstinence"*: William Hazlitt, "The Fight," in *Literary Remains of the Late William Hazlitt* (New York: Saunders and Otley, 1836), 223.

17   *"man of low birth"*: Fatal Effects of Gambling, op. cit., x.

18   *"dark idol"*: Thomas De Quincey, *Confessions of an English Opium-Eater* (Boston: James R. Osgood, 1873), 151.

18   *"that boy"*: Ibid., 18.

18   *"unfathomed"*: The Collected Writings of Thomas De Quincey (Edinburgh: Adam and Charles Black, 1890), III, 347.

18–19   *"I must premise"*: Confessions of an English Opium-Eater, op. cit., 151.

19   *"I went off"*: Ibid., 151–52.

19   *"violent biliousness"*: James Hogg, *De Quincey and His Friends* (London: Sampson Low, Marston, 1895), 213.

19   *"tossing and sleepless"*: Grevel Lindop, *The Opium-Eater: A Life of Thomas De Quincey* (New York: Taplinger, 1981), 258.

20   *"from one of Mr. Peacock's"*: "The Drama," in *The Harmonicum*, January 1823, 16.

20   *"I will take you to a better place"*: Walter Frith, "John Thurtell's Second Trial," in *The Monthly Review*, June 1907, 106.

20   *"It was the most dreadful"*: Ibid.

20–21   Ensor's account: Ibid., 105–07.

21   *"the warehouse is on fire"*: Ibid., 105.

23   *"one Saturday"*: Fatal Effects of Gambling, op. cit., 479.

24   *"keep a good look-out"*: A Complete History and Development of all the Extraordinary Circumstances and Events Connected with the Murder of Mr. Weare (London: Jones & Co., 1824), 250.

24   *"no doubt deterred"*: Fatal Effects of Gambling, op. cit., 483.

25   *"It was lucky for him"*: Ibid., 483.

25   *"Damn and blast Wood"*: Complete History and Development, op. cit., 248.

26   *"Mr. Weare, how are you?"*: Ibid., 250.

27   *"You dare not say a word"*: Narrative of the Mysterious and Dreadful Murder, op. cit., 9.

27 *"I do not forget this treatment"*: Complete History and Development, op. cit., 250.

27 *"clean and purify"*: Carlyle, Reminiscences, op. cit., 232.

27 *"Either the human being"*: De Quincey, Suspiria de Profundis (Edinburgh: Adam and Charles Black, 1879), 38.

27 *"with the foul"*: Carlyle, Reminiscences, op. cit., 179.

27 *"into effete Prose"*: Thomas Carlyle, "The Diamond Necklace," in Carlyle, Historical Essays (Berkeley: University of California Press, 2002), 136.

27 *"mystic deeps"*: Thomas Carlyle, Signs of The Times, in Guide to Carlyle (New York: Haskell House, 1920), 80.

28 *"suspend men from bed-posts"*: Carlyle, "The Diamond Necklace," op. cit., 136.

28 *"dim millions"*: Thomas Carlyle, History of Friedrich the Second Called Frederick the Great (New York: Collier, 1897), IV, 40.

28 *"poetical humbug"*: Thomas Moore, Letters and Journals of Lord Byron (Paris: Baudry's European Library, 1833), II, 443.

28 *"Sentence printed if not"*: The Correspondence of Thomas Carlyle and Ralph Waldo Emerson 1834–1872 (Boston: Ticknor, 1888), I, 93.

28 *"hieroglyphic page"*: Carlyle, "The Diamond Necklace," op. cit., 90.

29 *"I wish you would take a walk"*: Complete History and Development, op. cit., 7.

29 *"You made a bad business"*: Ibid., 252.

29 *"I know that"*: Ibid., 252.

29 *"on the spot"*: Ibid., 251.

29 *"You would de damned"*: Ibid., 252.

29 *"will you be in it"*: Fatal Effects of Gambling, op. cit., 176.

31 *"liquor up"*: Charles Hindley, The Life and Times of James Catnach (London: Reeves and Turner, 1878), 145.

31 *"A more silent"*: "Old Lyon's Inn," in Ballou's Monthly Magazine (July 1890) (Boston: Studley, 1890), LXXII, 43.

31 *"cards, hazard"*: Complete History and Development, op. cit., 251.

32 *Miss Malone*: The Trial of John Thurtell and Joseph Hunt (London: Sherwood, Jones, 1824), 30–31.

33 *"Have you got every thing"*: Complete History and Development, op. cit., 251.

34 *"I am sure"*: Fatal Effects of Gambling, op. cit., 492.

34 *"the chaise is ready"*: Ibid., 493.

34 *Cumberland Street*: Trial of John Thurtell, op. cit., 31.

35 *loin of pork*: Ibid., 23.

35 *"Here they are"*: Ibid., 16.

35 *"We know Jack is"*: Complete History and Development, op. cit., 255.

35 *"sing a good"*: Trial of John Thurtell, op. cit., 33.

36 *"You get out here"*: Fatal Effects of Gambling, op. cit., 494.

36 *Bow Street Horse Patrol*: Fairburn's Edition of the Whole Proceedings of the Trial of John Thurtell (London: John Fairburn, 1824), 37.

36 *landlord of the White Lion*: Trial of John Thurtell, op. cit., 32.

37 *stagnant water*: Honoré de Balzac, Lost Illusions, trans. Ellen Marriage (London: J. M. Dent, 1897), 44.

38   *"a charming"*: Lytton Strachey, *Portraits in Miniature and Other Essays* (London: Chatto & Windus, 1931), 70.

39   *"I then heard groans"*: *Fairburn's Edition of the Whole Proceedings*, op. cit., 39.

39   *"I had my wife"*: *Horrid Effects of Gambling Exemplified in the Atrocious Murder of Mr. Weare* (London: Hodgson, n.d.), 25.

41   *"He seemed to think"*: *Early Letters of Thomas Carlyle* (London: Macmillan, 1886), II, 230.

41   *"a loud, roaring"*: Carlyle, *Reminiscences*, op. cit., 122.

42   *"not only did more"*: John Ruskin, *Præterita* (Oxford: Oxford University Press, 1990), 6–7.

42   *"What sort of person was Mr. Weare?"*: In fact, this exchange seems not to have taken place during the trial. The historian Albert Borowitz believes that the writer had in mind a passage in the *Observer* of 2 November 1823, in which it was reported that Probert "always maintained an appearance of respectability, and kept his horse and gig." Percy Fitzgerald, in his *Chronicles of the Bow Street Police-Office*, points to a similar reference in the *Morning Chronicle*.

42   *"The gig of respectability"*: Carlyle, *Reminiscences*, op. cit., 190.

43   *"This is my friend Hunt"*: *Fatal Effects of Gambling*, op. cit., 495.

43   *"Now I'll take you"*: Ibid., 158.

43   *"hardly above five feet"*: Carlyle, *Reminiscences*, op. cit., 152.

44   drug-laden dreams: The images in this paragraph are derived from De Quincey, *Confessions of an English Opium-Eater*, op. cit.

44   *"was broad noon"*: Ibid., 120.

44   *"It is just by"*: *Fairburn's Edition of the Whole Proceedings*, op. cit., 25.

44   *"This is the place"*: Ibid.

45   *"This is all"*: Ibid.

45   *"As we were going"*: *Fatal Effects of Gambling*, op. cit., 496–97.

45   *"I never had"*: Ibid., 497.

45   *"like the devil"*: *Trial of John Thurtell*, op. cit., 18.

45–46 *"fought with me"*: *Fatal Effects of Gambling*, op. cit. 497.

46   *"about the jugular"*: *Trial of John Thurtell*, op. cit., 18.

46   *"jammed the pistol"*: Ibid.

47   *"hot from slaughtering"*: Borowitz, *Thurtell-Hunt Murder Case*, op. cit., 169.

48   *"as I have turned"*: *Complete History and Development*, op. cit., 258.

48   *"very cordially"*: Ibid.

48   *"You think me"*: Ibid.

48   *"tip them a stave"*: H. B. Irving, *A Book of Remarkable Criminals* (New York: Doran, 1918), 298.

50   *"world of ordinary life"*: *The Collected Writings of Thomas De Quincey* (London: A. C. Black, 1897), X, 392–94.

50   *"Hence it is"*: Ibid., 393.

51   Dionysian dowry: See Friedrich Nietzsche, *Ecce Homo*, trans. Walter Kaufmann (New York: Vintage, 1989), 266.

51   *"horrible mixture"*: Friedrich Nietzsche, *The Birth of Tragedy and The Case of Wagner*, trans. Walter Kaufmann (New York: Vintage, 1967), 39.

51   *"re-establishment"*: De Quincey, "On the Knocking at the Gate in *Macbeth*," op. cit., 393.

52   *"I suppose"*: *Complete History and Development*, op. cit., 258.

52   *"We may as well"*: Ibid.

53   *"That's your share"*: *Trial of John Thurtell*, op. cit., 18.

53   *"This is a bad"*: *Complete History and Development*, op. cit., 259.

54   *"mighty labyrinths"*: De Quincey, *Confessions of an English Opium-Eater*, op. cit., 59.

54   *Charles Lloyd*: Thomas De Quincey, *Literary Reminiscences* (Boston: Ticknor, Reed, and Fields, 1851), 157 et seq.

54   *"never to pay"*: De Quincey, "On the Knocking at the Gate in *Macbeth*," op. cit., 389.

55   *"the great alphabet"*: De Quincey, *Literary Reminiscences*, op. cit., 167.

55   *"sympathy must be"*: De Quincey, "On the Knocking at the Gate in *Macbeth*," op. cit., 391.

55   *"I think that would"*: *Trial of John Thurtell*, op. cit., 24.

55   *"You shall not"*: Ibid., 19.

56   *"very fine moonlight"*: *Horrid Effects of Gambling*, op. cit., 21.

56   *"heard something dragged"*: *Pierce Egan's Account of the Trial of John Thurtell and Joseph Hunt* (London: Knight & Lacey, 1824), 64.

56   *"hollow noise"*: *Horrid Effects of Gambling*, op. cit., 21.

57   *John Harrington*: *Pierce Egan's Account*, op. cit., 64; *Fairburn's Edition of the Whole Proceedings*, op. cit., 43; *Trial of John Thurtell*, op. cit., 11.

59   *"a great deal stained"*: *Complete History and Development*, op. cit., 262.

59   *"We Turpin lads"*: Ibid., 117.

59   *"would never do"*: *Fairburn's Edition of the Whole Proceedings*, op. cit., 35.

60   *"O John"*: *Complete History and Development*, op. cit., 262.

61   *"Then I'm baked"*: *Trial of John Thurtell*, op. cit., 20.

61   *"they can do nothing"*: *Fatal Effects of Gambling*, op. cit., 462.

62   *"will be better"*: *Fairburn's Edition of the Whole Proceedings*, op. cit., 27.

62   *"to pick up some"*: Lockhart, *Life of Sir Walter Scott*, op. cit., I, 115.

63   *"turns upon marvelous"*: Sir Walter Scott, "Romance," in *The Prose Works of Sir Walter Scott* (Paris: Galignani, 1827), V, 700.

63   *"exulting demoniac"*: Sir Walter Scott, *The Bride of Lamermoor* (London: Archibald Constable, 1895), 488.

63   *"a sort of romance"*: *Familiar Letters of Sir Walter Scott* (Edinburgh: David Douglas, 1894), 178.

63–64   *"I never saw"*: *The London and Paris Observer* (Paris: Galignani, 1857), 665.

64   *"Is that you, Jack"*: Egan, *Recollections of John Thurtell*, op. cit., 40.

64   *"John, my boy"*: Borowitz, *Thurtell-Hunt Murder Case*, op. cit., 36.

66   *"gentlemen of the first"*: *Fatal Effects of Gambling*, op. cit., 75.

66   *"it was pork"*: *Trial of John Thurtell*, op. cit., 36.

66   *"plum-colored frock-coat"*: Borowitz, *Thurtell-Hunt Murder Case*, op. cit., 143.

66   *"clung to every separate"*: Ibid., 173.

66   *"Cut me not off"*: Ibid.

67   *"strong desperate man"*: Edward Herbert, "A Pen and Ink Sketch of a Late Trial for Murder," in *Spirit of the English Magazines*, 1 April 1824. "Edward Herbert" was a pseudonym of John Hamilton Reynolds.

67   *"cannot but give"*: Complete History and Development, op. cit., 194–96.

67   *"all Sir Walter's"*: David Masson, "Thurtell's Murder of Weare," in *Select Essays of Thomas De Quincey Narrative & Imaginative* (Edinburgh: Adam and Charles Black, 1888), 180.

67–68 *"Very unsatisfactory"*: The Journal of Sir Walter Scott 1825–1832 (Edinburgh: David Douglas, 1891), 228.

68   *"strange intricate"*: Ibid., 607.

68   Scott's visit to the cottage: Ibid., 607–08.

68   *"Indeed the whole"*: Ibid.

68   *"took care always"*: Lockhart, *Life of Sir Walter Scott*, op. cit., IV, 63.

69   *"I am glad of it"*: "Prize-Fighting," in *The United Service Journal and Naval and Military Magazine* (January 1834) (London: Henry Colburn, 1834), 62–63.

69   *"since the calamitous"*: The Newgate Calendar (London: Robins and Co., 1828), IV, 402.

73   *Toward the end of December 1836*: Unless otherwise noted, all facts and quotations relating to The Mystery of the Mutilated Corpse have their source in (1) the transcript of the Trial of James Greenacre and Sarah Gale, April 1837, *Old Bailey Proceedings Online* (www.oldbaileyonline.org, version 6.0, 17 April 2011) (t18370403-917), (2) "Edgware-Road Tragedy," in *Annual Register*, April 1837, 37–42, or (3) the entry for James Greenacre in *Dictionary of National Biography* (New York: Macmillan, 1890), XXIII, 61 et seq.

74   *"like to His glorious body"*: Philippians 3:21.

77   *"It was what"*: "The Edgware Road Murder," in *The London Medical and Surgical Journal* (London: Michael Ryan *et alia*, 1837), I, 62.

80   *"hardly light enough"*: New Letters of Thomas Carlyle (London: John Lane, 1904), I, 53.

80   *"Only once!"*: Matthew Arnold, "Samuel Taylor Coleridge," in *The English Poets*, ed. T. H. Ward (New York and London: Macmillan, 1894), IV, 111.

82   *Crimley Hall*: Kimberley Hall, in fact; but the name came to be spelled as it was pronounced. The pedigree which traces the descent of the Wodehouses from Sir Constantine de Wodehouse, a knight who in the reign of Henry I is said to have married an heiress of the Botetorts, has been pronounced spurious by at least one genealogist. See Walter Rye, "Doubtful Norfolk Pedigrees," in *The Genealogist* (London: George Bell, 1879), 129–32. The specious derivation would perhaps have amused the most illustrious of the family's scions, P. G. Wodehouse.

83   *"womb that never bare"*: The Annotated Book of Common Prayer (London: Longmans, Green, 1907), 283.

83–84 *"remarkable peculiarity"*: Patriot, 13 April 1837.

87   *"an ocean that no"*: Honoré de Balzac in Twenty-Five Volumes (New York: Peter Fenelon Collier & Son, 1900), XV, 350.

87   *"ghosts in the open air"*: Baudelaire, "Les Sept vieillards."

87   *his sister's landlady*: Max Décharné, *Capital Crimes: Seven Centuries of London Life and Murder* (London: Arrow, 2013), 214.

88   *Mr. Gay's inquiries*: Décharné, *Capital Crimes*, op. cit., 214.

89   *north wind: New Letters of Thomas Carlyle*, op. cit., I, 48.

90   *"countenance presented": The Chronicles of Crime* (London: Reeves and Turner, 1886), II, 433.

92   *"Babel din"*: Wordsworth, *The Prelude*, quoted in John Williams, *Wordsworth: Romantic Poetry and Revolutionary Politics* (Manchester: Manchester University Press, 1989), 123.

92   *"such a silence": New Letters of Thomas Carlyle*, op. cit., I, 48.

93   *"enlightened Philosophism"*: Thomas Carlyle, *The French Revolution* (London: Chapman and Hall, 1896), I, 4.

93   *"algebraic spectralities"*: James Anthony Froude, *Thomas Carlyle: A History of His Life in London 1834–1881* (London: Longmans, Green, 1890), II, 359.

93   *"sometimes insane"*: Richard Garnett, *Life of Ralph Waldo Emerson* (London: Walter Scott, 1888), 66.

93   *"Gorgons, and Hydras"*: Charles Lamb, "Witches, and Other Night Fears," in *The Works of Charles Lamb* (New York: Crowell, 1882), III, 114.

94   *"What are you about": Lives of the Most Notorious and Daring Highwaymen, Robbers, and Murderers* (London: Milner, n.d.), 270.

98   *"seemed quite unconcerned": Chronicles of Crime*, op. cit., II, 432.

99   *some few sages*: When James Boswell said that the philosopher David Hume professed to contemplate his own mortality with equanimity, Dr. Johnson replied, "Sir, if he really thinks so, his perceptions are disturbed; he is mad: if he does not think so, he lies." Boswell then said that the actor Samuel Foote told him that "he was not afraid to die." "It is not true, sir," Johnson said. "Hold a pistol to Foote's breast, or to Hume's breast, and threaten to kill them, and you'll see how they behave."

100   *"for this fraud": Lives of the Most Notorious and Daring Highwaymen, Robbers and Murderers Compiled from Authentic Sources* (Manchester: S. Johnson, 1844), 349.

101   *"injured Englishman"*: Ibid., 353.

101   *"generous public"*: Ibid., 351.

101   *"Wanted, a partner": Chronicles of Crime*, op. cit., II, 450.

103   *resumed their walks: The Spectator* (1 April 1837) (London: Joseph Clayton, 1837), X, 291.

104   *"command at any time": Chronicles of Crime*, op. cit., II, 435.

104   *"feigned laugh"*: Ibid.

104   *"alarmed me"*: Ibid.

104   *"I thought it might"*: Ibid.

104   *"safest and most prudent": The Spectator* (1 April 1837), op. cit., X, 291.

105   *Sarah Gale: Chronicles of Crime*, op. cit., II, 452.

105   *"bucket and mop"*: Joseph Forster, *Studies in Red and Black* (London: Ward and Downey, 1896), 205.

106   *"This female": Chronicles of Crime*, op. cit., II, 435.

106   *"eleven sovereigns": Lives of the Most Notorious* (1844), op. cit., 365.

108   *"truly right-minded"*: "Memoir of Mr. Justice Coltman," in *The Law Magazine* (London: W. Benning, 1849), XI, 298.

108   *John Adolphus*: "Mr. J. Adolphus," *The Illustrated London News*, 26 July 1845, 64; James Grant, *Portraits of Public Characters* (London: Saunders

and Otley, 1841), 217 et seq.; *The Gentleman's Magazine* (September 1845) (London: John Bower Nichols, 1845), XXIV, 315; William Ballantine, *Some Experiences of a Barrister's Life* (New York: Henry Holt, 1882), 71.

109   *"perfectly indifferent"*: Chronicles of Crime, op. cit., II, 439.

111   *Blackstone*: Sir William Blackstone, *Commentaries on the Laws of England* (New York: Banks and Brothers, 1884), 1035 et seq.

112   *"cared nothing for death"*: Chronicles of Crime, op. cit., II, 445.

112   *"enraged at the deception"* Even after his admission to the sheriffs, Greenacre continued to insist that he was not guilty of murder. When the Rev. Dr. Cotton, the Newgate chaplain, spoke of him as a murderer (in the "condemned sermon" he preached in Newgate chapel two days before the execution), Greenacre took offense and denied that the term could with justice be applied to him. In this he was certainly mistaken. A man who, without a considerable provocation, beats a person so that the person dies is guilty of murder whether or not he intended the person's death: "he is guilty," says Blackstone, "of murder by express malice; that is, by an express evil design," for "no person, unless of an abandoned heart, would be guilty of such an act, upon a slight or no apparent cause." If, however, the killer can prove that he acted upon a sufficient provocation, he is not guilty of murder. A man so provoked that he kills another man "by beating him in such a manner as shewed only an intent to chastise and not to kill him" is not a murderer in the eyes of the law, which "so far considers the provocation of contumelious behaviour, as to adjudge it only manslaughter, and not murder." The provocation in question, however, *must be something more than hard or taunting words*: "No affront, by words or gestures only, is a sufficient provocation, so as to excuse or extenuate such acts of violence as manifestly endanger the life of another."

112   *told the sheriffs*: : Ibid., 441.

113   *"pain which is essential"*: Arthur Schopenhauer, *The World as Will and Idea*, trans. R. B. Haldane and J. Kemp (London: Kegan Paul, 1906–07), I, 406.

114   *"summoned enchantment"*: Ibid., II, 9.

114   *"renunciation"*: "Autobiography of a Mystic," in *The Church Quarterly Review* (October 1898) (London: Spottiswoode, 1899), XLVII, 186.

114   *"be given"*: Schopenhauer, *The World as Will and Idea*, op. cit., III, 423.

115   *"cadaverous perfume"*: Nietzsche, *Ecce Homo*, op. cit., 270.

115   *"a place of quite"*: Schopenhauer, *The World as Will and Idea*, op. cit., III, 456.

116   *"kissed the rope"*: Ibid., III, 457.

116   *"Still more remarkable"*: Ibid., III, 456–57.

116   *"fanatical delusion"*: Ibid., III, 457.

116   *"presence of a violent"*: Ibid., III, 455–56.

118   *"state of beastly"*: The Spectator (6 May 1837), op. cit., X, 416.

118   *"smoking, drinking"*: Diary of Sir Michael Connal (Glasgow: James MacLehose, 1895), 9.

119   *"Gentlemen"*: George Tancred, *Rulewater and Its People* (Edinburgh: Constable, 1907), 129.

120   *"The dog died game"*: John Heneage Jesse, *George Selwyn and His Contemporaries* (London: Richard Bentley, 1843), I, 354.

120   *"was death's counterfeit"*: Arthur Griffiths, *The Chronicles of Newgate* (London: Chapman and Hall, 1884), 425.

120–121   *"became as abject"*: Andrew Knapp and William Baldwin, *The New New-gate Calendar* (London: Gunder, n.d.), III, 165.

121   *"Encore un moment"*: "She was so terrified," Dostoevsky has Lebedev say in *The Idiot*, "that she did not understand what was happening. But when Samson [Charles-Henri Sanson, the executioner] seized her head, and pushed her under the knife with his foot, she cried out: 'Wait a moment! wait a moment, monsieur!' Well, because of that moment of bitter suffering, perhaps the Saviour will pardon her other faults, for one cannot imagine a greater agony."

122   *"'Neath the timbers"*: *Punch* (London: Punch, 1849), XVII, 210.

123   *"was totally unmanned"*: "Execution of Greenacre," in *Annual Register* (May 1837) (London: Rivington, 1838), 45.

123   *"great self-possession"*: See the entry on Greenacre in *The Oxford Dictionary of National Biography*.

123   *"Don't leave me"*: Ibid.

123   *"Ten different witnesses"*: Carlyle, *French Revolution*, op. cit., III, 110.

125   *"quivering in mortal"*: Charles Kingston, *Remarkable Rogues* (London: John Lane, 1921), 195.

125   *"The question of motive"*: *The Trial of Mary Blandy*, ed. William Roughead (Project Gutenberg, 2004).

129   *essay on Sir Walter Scott*: Thomas Carlyle, "Sir Walter Scott," in Carlyle, *Critical and Miscellaneous Essays* (London: Chapman and Hall, 1899), IV, 22–24.

130   *"Veneration of great men"*: Ibid., IV, 24.

131   *lion-soirées*: Ibid., IV, 23.

131   *"I was charmed"*: *The Collected Letters of Thomas Carlyle and Jane Welsh Carlyle* (Durham, North Carolina: Duke University Press, 1990), XVI, 19–24.

131   *"he never had a first love"*: Hershel Parker, *The Powell Papers: A Confidence Man Amok among the Anglo-American Literati* (Evanston: Northwestern University Press, 2011), 276.

132   *"first beloved"*: Plato, Lysis 219c-d.

132   *"was more to be pitied"*: Parker, *Powell Papers*, op. cit., 276.

132–133   *"one of those persons"*: Peter Gay, *The Naked Heart: The Bourgeois Experience: Victoria to Freud* (New York: Norton, 1996), 182.

133   *"trenchant opinions"*: Gertrude Himmelfarb, *Marriage and Morals among the Victorians and Other Essays* (New York: Vintage, 1987), 13. And yet if Jane was not indeed the victim Carlyle made her out be—if she was not in fact laid a sacrifice on the altar of his genius—the fact that he should portray her as such argues a degree of self-absorption in Carlyle himself that might well have made for strains in a marriage. That he should transform the ordinary ups and downs of wedded life into a Greek tragedy that it wasn't suggests that he was less interested in what his wife actually was than what, in his idealized conception of himself, she should have been. What a dereliction, in a hero-prophet, to have had a happy domestic life!

134   *"entirely miserable"*: James Anthony Froude, *My Relations with Carlyle* (London: Longman's Green, 1903), 11.

134   *"The chief interest"*: Jane Welsh Carlyle's Journal, October 1855–July 1856, in *The Collected Letters of Thomas Carlyle and Jane Welsh Carlyle,* op. cit., XXX, 259.

134   *"realised what a tragedy"*: Froude, *My Relations with Carlyle,* op. cit., 13.

135   *Through the agency of Froude*: A leaf from Jane Carlyle's diary for June 1856 and four lines from the succeeding leaf are missing from the manuscript; they were possibly removed by Carlyle's niece, Mary Aitken. The story of the "bluemarks" did not appear during Froude's life; he related it in an essay, "Relations with Carlyle," which was published by his children as a book, *My Relations with Carlyle,* op. cit., after his death.

139   *throat was cut*: Unless otherwise noted, all facts and quotations concerning The Murder in Mayfair have their source in (1) the transcript of the Trial of François Benjamin Courvoisier, June 1840, *Old Bailey Proceedings Online* (www.oldbaileyonline.org, version 6.0, 17 April 2011) (t18400615-1629) or (2) Lord William Russell (1767–1840), www.historyofparliamentonline.org / volume/1820-1832/member/russell-lord-william-1767-1840.

140   *"adequate for"*: Diary of John Adolphus, quoted in Yseult Bridges, *Two Studies in Crime* (London: Hutchinson, 1959), 65.

144   *"Sovereignty of the People"*: *The Spectator* (January 28, 1837), op. cit., X, 74.

151   *towel and bedclothes*: Tedman maintained that *he* had removed the towel from Lord William's face. His memory might have misled him; Dr. Elsgood might have replaced the towel; or Tedman may have wished others to believe—may have wished himself to believe—that the police had been on the scene before the surgeon. Young, Mr. Latham's butler, a presumably disinterested witness, distinctly "saw the napkin taken off his lordship by Mr. Elsgood, the surgeon."

154   *"a damned bore"*: *The Greville Memoirs* (London: Longmans, Green, 1905–07), III, 126.

154   *"most shocking"*: *The Letters of Queen Victoria,* ed. A. C. Benson and Viscount Esher (New York: Longmans, Green, 1907), 278.

155   *"The bed was"*: Ibid., 279.

156   *"Visionary servants"*: *Greville Memoirs,* op. cit., IV, 293.

157   *"wholly unaware"*: Edward Harold Begbie, *The Mirrors of Downing Street* (New York: G. P. Putnam's Sons, 1921), 67.

160–161   *"The circumstances"*: *Greville Memoirs,* op. cit., IV, 293.

161   *"no evidence"*: Ibid., 294.

161   *"He is rather"*: Ibid., 293–94.

163   *Lord Wriothesley Russell*: Lord William Russell's daughter, Eliza Laura Henrietta, married her first cousin, Lord Wriothesley Russell.

163   *obsequies of Lord William*: *The Tablet,* 16 May 1840.

164   *"very pale"*: *Annual Register* (1840) (London: Rivington, 1841), 230.

165   *"Not guilty"*: Ibid., 230.

165   *"for they imagined"*: Bridges, *Two Studies in Crime,* op. cit., 73.

166   *"heavily in favour"*: Ibid., 78.

166   *"he appeared"*: *The Times,* 20 June 1840.

166   *"a communication of the facts"*: Bridges, *Two Studies in Crime*, op. cit., 93.

166   *"Let us have"*: The Times, 20 June 1840.

166   *"Call Charlotte"*: Bridges, *Two Studies in Crime*, op. cit., 93.

166   *"the greatest composure"*: Ibid., 93–94.

168   *"Tell Mr. Phillips"*: Punch, op. cit., XVII, 223.

170   *"Of course, then"*: The Gentleman's Magazine (November 1850) (John Bowyer Nichols, 1850), XXXIV, 524.

170   *"extremely eloquent"*: Ballantine, *Some Experiences*, op. cit., 78.

171   *Disraeli:* Michael Knox Beran, "Disraeli's Ghost," *The Claremont Review of Books*, Summer 2012, 35–37.

172   *"absolute martyrdom"*: Thomas Carlyle, *On Heroes, Hero-Worship, and the Heroic in History* (Boston: Ginn, 1901), xlviii.

172   *"scheme of Courvoisier"*: Thomas De Quincey, "Three Memorable Murders" (1854), in De Quincey, *The Note-Book of an English Opium-Eater and Miscellaneous Essays* (Boston: James Osgood, 1873), 62.

173   *"sullen and reserved"*: "Curious Trials connected with the Aristocracy," in *The Patrician* (London: Churton, 1848), VI, 246.

174   *"ought always to go"*: *Report of the Trial of Courvoisier* (Chiswick: Chiswick Press, 1918), 112; *The Spectator* (27 June 1840) (London: Joseph Clayton, 1840), XIII, 609.

174–175   *"This was the first"*: Ibid.

175   *"is his friend"*: Bridges, *Two Studies in Crime*, op. cit., 110.

176   *"different scenes"*: The Examiner, 12 July 1840.

176   *"to premeditate"*: Ibid.

176   *"history of thieves"*: Ibid.

176   *"be better concealed"*: Ibid.

177   *"had some altercation"*: Ibid.

177   *"When I opened"*: Ibid.

179   *"O God!"*: Bridges, *Two Studies in Crime*, op. cit., 117.

179   *"whether he was fully"*: The Examiner, 12 July 1840.

179   *"There it stands"*: Bridges, *Two Studies in Crime*, op. cit., 113 *et seq.*

180   *"was wont to say"*: John Aubrey, *"Brief Lives"* (Oxford: Clarendon Press, 1898), I, 111.

180   *"possible he could"*: Bridges, *Two Studies in Crime*, op. cit., 120–21.

181   *"immense sway"*: Ibid., 115 *et seq.*

181   *"was steady"*: Ibid., 118.

181   *"turned his head"*: Ibid., 116.

185   *"much overrated"*: Thomas De Quincey, "On Murder Considered as One of the Fine Arts," in *Select Essays of Thomas De Quincey Narrative & Imaginative,* ed. David Masson (Edinburgh: Adam and Charles Black, 1888), 56.

185   *"supremacy above all"*: De Quincey, "Three Memorable Murders," op. cit., 5.

186   *"scenical features"*: Ibid., 4.

186   *"most chaotic"*: Ibid., 8.

186   *"the sure receptacle"*: Ibid., 9.

187   *"Exceeding darkness"*: Ibid., 14.

188   *"stationary"*: Ibid., 18.

188   *"We know of it"*: P. D. James and T. A. Critchley, *The Maul and the Pear Tree: The Ratcliffe Highway Murders 1811* (New York: Mysterious Press, 1986), 13.

188   *"She had no fear"*: De Quincey, "Three Memorable Murders," op. cit., 22.

188   *"rang the bell"*: Ibid., 23.

188–189   *"that led downwards"*: Ibid., 24.

189   *"one, two, three"*: Ibid.

189   *"Mr. Marr!"*: James and Critchley, *The Maul and the Pear Tree*, op. cit., 13.

189   *"Marr, Marr"*: Ibid., 14.

189   *"so floated with gore"*: De Quincey, "Three Memorable Murders," op. cit., 27.

191   *"frenzy of feelings"*: Ibid., 5–6.

192   *"You are an officer"*: *The Examiner*, 22 December 1811.

192   *"I certainly will"*: James and Critchley, *The Maul and the Pear Tree*, op. cit., 66.

192   *"white as a corpse's"*: "Some Curiosities of Crime," in *Otago Witness*, 2 June 1892.

192   *"There's murder inside"*: Ibid.

192   *"dreadful annunciation"*: De Quincey, "Three Memorable Murders," op. cit., 55.

193   *"the wolfish dog"*: Ibid., 56.

195   *"suspended by the neck"*: James and Critchley, *The Maul and the Pear Tree*, op. cit., 128.

196   *"objective correlative"*: T. S. Eliot, "Hamlet," in Eliot, *Selected Essays* (San Diego: Harcourt Brace Jovanovich, 1950), 124 et seq.

198   *"Damn you"*: Martin Baggoley, *Surrey Executions* (Stroud: Amberley Publishing, 2013) (electronic edition).

199   *"Monsieur can never"*: Sabine Baring-Gould, *The Book of Were-Wolves* (London: Smith, Elder, 1865), 2.

199   *"ghastly and revolting"*: Ibid., 131.

201   *"bloodhound"*: De Quincey, "Three Memorable Murders," op. cit., 19, 56, 11.

201   *"of the most extraordinary"*: Ibid., 9–10.

201   *"cadaverous"*: Ibid., 37.

202   *"unnatural"*: Ibid., 34.

202   *"début"*: De Quincey, "On Murder Considered as One of the Fine Arts" (Supplementary Paper), op. cit., 72.

202   *Titian*: Ibid., 11.

203   *"with an insatiate"*: Edward Gibbon, *The History of the Decline and Fall of the Roman Empire* (New York: De Fau, 1906), I, 109.

203   *"villainously pranked"*: *The Works of Charles Lamb* (New York: A. C. Armstrong, 1886), III, v.

203   *"All perils"*: De Quincey, "Three Memorable Murders," op. cit., 34.

204   *"gathering agitation"*: Thomas De Quincey, "A Sequel to the Confessions," in De Quincey, *Confessions of an English Opium-Eater*, op. cit., 148.

206   Mary Ann *"Polly"* Nichols: *The Times*, 1 September 1888.

208   *"one of the worst"*: *The Times*, 11 April 1863.

208   *"to get a young woman"*: Ibid.

209   *Emma Jackson*: Ibid.

212   *Ann Priest*: Nicola Sly, *Oxfordshire Murders* (Stroud: History Press, 2012) (electronic book).

214   *decent obscurity*: Compare Gibbon: "My English text is chaste, and all licentious passages are left in the obscurity of a learned language."

214   *outrage to her womanhood*: The post-mortem examination conducted by Professor Kidd of the University together with three surgeons found that her "death resulted from blood loss following insertion of either a sharp instrument or a blunt and powerful instrument into her vagina, the instrument having been violently jiggled in different directions, causing deep cuts." Sly, *Oxfordshire Murders*, op. cit.

215   *had never been*: E. M. Darlington, *The Radcliffes of Leigh Lancashire: A Family Memorial* (privately printed, 1918).

217   *"is a dull dog"*: Arthur Machen, *The Great God Pan and The Inmost Light* (London: John Lane, 1895), 116.

225   *"will forget the terror"*: Sir Melville L. Macnaghten, *Days of My Years* (New York: Longmans, Green, 1914), 55.

225–226 *Nichols and Chapman*: Ibid., 58.

226   *"Dear Boss" letter*: Ibid.

226   *Stride and Eddowes*: Ibid., 59–60.

226–227 *Mary Jane Kelley*: Ibid., 60–61; "The 'Crank' or Criminal of Whitechapel," in *The Alienist and Neurologist* (St. Louis: Carreras, 1889), X, 102–04.

227   *"too apathetic"*: Augusta Larned, "Whitechapel, London," in *The Freemason's Repository* (July 1889) (Providence: E. L. Freeman and Son, 1888–89), XVIII, 507.

227   *"the fury"*: Macnaghten, *Days of My Years*, op. cit., 61.

229   *"quite sure"*: Arthur Symons, *The Symbolist Movement in Literature* (New York: E. P. Dutton, 1919), 5.

230   *"away from Whitechapel"*: *The Letters of Henry James*, ed. Percy Lubbock (New York: Scribner's Sons, 1920), I, 141.

230   *"detestable summer"*: Ibid., 140.

231   *"Mr. Jones"*: Joseph Conrad, *Victory* (Garden City: Doubleday, 1915), 81–82, 90–93, 95–96.

234   *"to be curious"*: De Quincey, "On Murder," op. cit., 10.

234   *Stephen on murder*: Leslie Stephen, "The Decay of Murder," in *The Cornhill Magazine* (London: Smith, Elder & Co., 1869), XX, 722–733.

236   *Wilson on murder*: Edmund Wilson, "Why Do People Read Detective Stories?" (October 14, 1944), in Wilson, *Classics and Commercials: A Literary Chronicle of the Forties* (New York: Farrar, Straus and Giroux, 1950), 231–37.

Index